Copyright © historyofwrestling.info 2015. All Rights Reserved.

Published by lulu.com

All rights reserved. This book may not be reproduced, in whole or in any part, in any form, without written permission from the publisher or author.

This book is set in Rockwell Extra Bold, Impact and Arial.

10 9 8 7 6 5 4 3 2 1

This book was printed and bound in the United Kingdom.

THE HEAT FILES 1998

James Dixon
Arnold Furious
Lee Maughan
Rick Ashley
Bob Dahlstrom

THE HEAT FILES 1998

MEET THE TEAM

All of the contributors in this book have been wrestling fans for a long time, probably longer than we would care to admit. Some of our favourite memories of our early wrestling fandom involved renting video tapes and watching them repeatedly. However, there had never been one truly all encompassing guide to those tapes, and what turns up on them. Yes, there are some great sites on the internet here and there, but nothing ever published. No guide book. Here at *History of Wrestling*, we decided that *we* would write that book, and we did! With a century of combined viewing between us, we have lived through all of this many times over. We decided to bring that knowledge and love of wrestling, to you. While the opinions you will read are often controversial, off-the-wall or just plain moronic, they are from likeminded people who put wrestling before almost anything else. Disagree with them if you wish, certainly the office has seen its fair share of furniture thrown and occasional bloodshed (there was an unpleasant incident with a stapler that was later resolved with a pint). After the success of our ongoing *Complete WWF Video Guide* series, and the fun we had doing it, we have decided to branch out further and cover *everything* the WWF has ever produced. It might take a while. This is the first in our series of books covering WWF B-show show Sunday Night Heat. Look out for other TV shows and books about other wrestling promotions, coming soon.

THE TEAM AT WWW.HISTORYOFWRESTLING.INFO:

ARNOLD FURIOUS

Arnold Furious likes... Mitsuharu Misawa, Jushin Liger, Eddy Guerrero, Bret Hart, Raven, Toshiaki Kawada, Vader, Samoa Joe, Bryan Danielson, Kenta Kobashi, Star Wars, Martin Scorsese, Arnold Schwarzenegger, Bill Hicks, Wall-E, Akira Kurosawa, Johnny Cash, Scott Pilgrim, Tintin, The Wire, Firefly, The Simpsons, Jackie Chan, AC/DC, Rocky, Simon Furman, Danny Wallace, Aerosmith, The British Red Cross, Garth Ennis, Batman, Kiss, Asterix, Alan Moore's Top Ten, Astor City, Christopher Waken, Juliette and the Licks, Quentin Tarantino, Goodfellas, Kurt Busiek, Watchmen (the book, not the film), White Out (the book, not the film), Super Troopers, Swingers, Death's Head, Iron Maiden, Will Ferrell, Clint Eastwood, Trish Stratus, Everton FC, Tom Hanks, The Blues Brothers, Simon Pegg, Clerks, Terry Pratchett, Richard Pryor, Viz, Mutemath, Joe Bonamassa, How to Train Your Dragon, Stevie Ray Vaughan, Dexter, Jimi Hendrix, Alien, Aliens, Predator, Frankie Boyle, Secret Wars, Woody Allen, True Romance, Lethal Weapon, Takashi Miike, Graham Linehan, Big Bang Theory, Darren Aronofsky, John Woo, Charlie Chaplin, films with ridiculous shoot-out sequences in them, Douglas Adams, Chow Yun Fat, 12 Angry Men, Wilson Pickett, Studio Ghibli, Pixar, The Avengers, Fable II, history, Bill Bailey, Skyrim, Stephen Fry, Top Gear, kung fu movies, Alan Wake, Meet the Feebles, Die Hard, Sin City (the books and the film), zombies, Red Dwarf, Peter Sellers, Peter Cook, Michael Caine, Planet of the Apes, conspiracies, steak, The Princess Bride, Grimlock, Mel Brooks, top fives, 30 Rock, Preacher, Pringles, Pirates of the Caribbean, Back to the Future, Klaus Kinski, The Sopranos, boxing, Casablanca, Stephen King, Hunter S. Thompson, Mike Leigh's Naked, Captain America, Hawkeye, Spaced, Flight of the Conchords, Monty Python, Pearl Jam, Carol Danvers, 100 Bullets, Indiana Jones, The Goon, Thorntons, Jack Nicholson, Jim Beam, real ale, cartoons, novelty underwear, the Joker, Frank Miller, Robert Brockway, The Breakfast Club, Far Cry 3, Freddy Krueger, Alec Baldwin's speech in Glengarry Glen Ross, John Carpenter, Bill & Ted, MMA, John Wayne, Terrence Howard, The Terminator, Guy Forsyth, nudity, coffee, crazy Japanese films that make no sense, crazy Japanese wrestling that makes no sense, crazy Japanese people that make no sense, Greg Benson, Tony Cottam, Bernard Rage, Redje Harris, Ezet Samalca...and forever Maria.

JAMES DIXON

James Dixon has been watching wrestling for over 20 years. Inspired by the likes of Davey Boy Smith, Bret Hart and The Undertaker, Dixon was drawn to the business like any other fan, for reasons that are difficult to explain. A hobby quickly became an obsession, and Dixon was determined to get involved in wrestling by utilising the one thing he could do: write about it. In previous books James wrote alongside his "writing partner" Evil Ste. The truth is, the Evil Ste character was merely an extension of Dixon's own personality, his way of sharing his Jekyll and Hyde opinions on things. The writing choice worked fairly well at first, but the team all feel it has perhaps become more gimmicky that was hoped, so Dixon has reverted to just writing as himself. Well, we say himself. In reality James is a former British professional wrestler, but he has adopted the pseudonym to retain relative anonymity and to distance himself from his past career in the industry. However, that past experience does give him a unique and more inside perspective on things than the others, though he is still a "mark" at heart. James has limited patience for anything in wrestling post-2002, and much prefers 80s and 90s grappling. Curious really, because as you will see in these pages, he spends a lot of time complaining about it. James currently lives in the North of England, where it rains the majority if the time.

LEE MAUGHAN

Lee Maughan has been a fan of the professional wrestling industry for as long has he can remember, dating back to an embryonic memory of sitting on his grandparent's living room floor, his eyes transfixed to British household names Big Daddy and Giant Haystacks belly-busting their way through ITV's *World of Sport*. Somehow this wasn't enough to deter him, and young Lee was rewarded with having the incredibly good fortune to be within the WWF's target demographic just in time its early 90s UK boom period. He was hooked, his bedroom quickly becoming a wall-to-wall palace of video tapes, action figures, magazines, posters and any piece of tat all stamped with the WWF insignia. His thirst for the quasi-sport was ravenous but unfortunately, his family were too cheap to subscribe to Sky television, home of the WWF. His quencher? WCW *International Pro*, broadcast well past his bedtime on regional terrestrial station Tyne-Tees. Those WWF magazines soon found themselves piled up alongside copies of *Pro Wrestling Illustrated* and *Superstars of Wrestling*, making Lee possibly the most clued-up eight year old wrestling superfan in the entire TS14 postcode. It's possible, nay probable thanks to a further 20 years of research, that Lee is still the most clued-up wrestling superfan in the entire TS14 postcode. A trader of tapes, a distributor of DVDs and a purveyor of pixels, Lee keeps up with everything from New Japan to CHIKARA whilst continuing to catch up with the classics of pro wrestling's territorial days. Away from the grapple game, Lee likes to watch sitcoms, rock out in punk bands, and play video games with a strong preference for old school platformers and kart racers. Despite this, he even found the time to graduate from the University of Teesside in 2005 with a degree in media production, and after much soul searching and stints making Christmas cards for a living and working as a producer and on-air talent for a community radio station, is now taking the tentative first steps into the world of film video editing. He also tweets with a reverently dry sense of humour **@atomicbombs**, but reserves the right to ignore you entirely unless you want to pay him to write about wrestling, guitar bands or 80s pop culture for your book, website or magazine.

BOB DAHLSTROM

Bob Dahlstrom is many things. A son, a brother, an uncle; but also is a dude who likes to draw. And more importantly than that, a lifelong wrestling fan. It all started back at WrestleMania III, which hooked young Bob. He would then go onto rent every wrestling tape from every video rental place around, and watch them over and over. He's never looked back. All the artwork in this book has been loving crafted exclusively by Bob, specially for this publication. He lives in Illinois with his girlfriend and pet guinea pig. His wrestling artwork and autobiographical webcomic *Egomaniac* can be found at www.robertpfd.com.

Follow us on Facebook:
www.facebook.com/historyofwrestling.info

Follow us on Twitter:
@HOWwrestling

THE SCORING SYSTEM

We have used the popular star system in order to rate the matches that appear in this book. For those who are unaware of it, here is the key:

*****	Perfect
****½	Very close to perfect
****	Superb
***½	Very good
***	Good
**½	Decent
**	Average
*½	Nothing to it
*	Bad
½*	Terrible
DUD	Utterly worthless
SQUASH	Not rated (too short)
N/R	Not rated (for various reasons)
Negatives	Any match that goes into negative stars is one of the worst you will ever see

Sometimes things will be so bad, that we go into negative stars. These are matches that will make you want to stop watching wrestling and find a new hobby. We also dabble frequently in quarter stars, just when we cannot quite decide which of the above criteria a match falls under, and decide that it is somewhere in between.

It is important to remember that all star ratings are entirely subjective to the person awarding them. One man's **** bout could be another man's **. There is no set judging system for these things, this is not gymnastics or synchronised diving. That is the uniqueness of wrestling; everyone likes it for different reasons. There have been a few times in the past that the writers have reviewed the same matches and given different ratings. This is an example of how different people perceive things. So if your favourite match is not rated as highly as you might have hoped, don't worry, it shouldn't change your enjoyment of it. In fact, many a good natured argument has occurred in our offices about whether a match is "*****" or ****¾", that is just the nature of the business and one of the things that makes it so unique and fun to watch.

Some may also be wondering how we reached the scores that each show receives at the end of a review. Rest assured, it is not just a figure plucked out of the sky, like in some video games magazines. Rather, we have created a complex algorithm that takes into account various factors and data. These include: length of the show, the ratings of the matches (and segments) broken down into weighted points that are awarded to the show, the number of matches, historical relevance, and many other factors. Unfortunately this is top secret, and we cannot go into a full explanation here. However, we can guarantee that many hours have been spent on this in order to make it the fairest and most consistent overall review scoring system you will ever find. Of course, you can still get the opinion of the writers about whether it is worth seeing, regardless of the score, in the verdict section of the review.

The score it produces is not so much an overall rating for the show, but rather a "watchability" rating. Basically, how easy it is to sit through in one sitting and enjoy. Some shows have genuine, all-time classic matches, on long cards full of dull wrestling otherwise. While that match will improve the score of the show, it alone is not enough to make the whole show watchable on its own. The match yes, the show no.

Some tapes, shows and events inevitably end up with very high scores, and can even surpass the 100 point limit that we set. Our cap is 100, so that is the highest score a card can get. Similarly, a show can drop below zero if it is so bad, but we cap the minimum at zero so it cannot. If something receives a full 100 score, it does not necessarily mean that all of the content is perfect. Rather, as a whole, it is generally so good and consistent and in places outstanding, that it is entirely watchable and the time flies by when viewing it. These scores crop up now and again, but not too frequently. The score is the overall equivalent of a 5* match. In our eyes at least, anyway.

A complete list of the shows in order of score is available at the back of the book.

We have made attempts to be a little more generous with the ratings we awarded to matches in this book, as compared to say a pay-per-view event or home video release. This is because the content offered here was available for free on TV, and thus you are not paying to watch the bout. That in itself can sometimes be enough to turn a ** match on PPV into a *** match on TV.

CONTENTS

AUGUST

10	08.02.98
13	08.09.98
15	08.16.98
17	08.23.98
21	08.30.98

SEPTEMBER

23	09.06.98
25	09.13.98
27	09.20.98
31	09.27.98

OCTOBER

33	10.04.98
36	10.11.98
39	10.18.98
42	10.25.98

NOVEMBER

44	11.01.98
47	11.08.98
50	11.15.98
52	11.22.98
55	11.29.98

DECEMBER

57	12.06.98
60	12.13.98
61	12.20.98
63	12.27.98

66	Television Classics
66	Hall of Shame
67	The Story So Far...
68	Heat Recap Summary

08.02.98 by James Dixon
Venue: Anaheim, CA
Taped: 07.27.98
TV Rating: 3.7

Welcome to *Sunday Night HeAT*, the WWF's short-running weekly Sunday television show. With the company riding a wave of previously unseen success in 1998 thanks to the rise of Steve Austin, The Rock, DX and a number of others, their viewing public demanded further satiation than the weekly two-hour *RAW* episodes they were getting. The WWF responded with the creation of this show, offering fresh, first-run programming that could serve as a vehicle to further angles and set the scene for the next night's *RAW* broadcast. Unlike *Shotgun Saturday Night*, with which they tried something similar two years ago, this has no gimmicks. It is just another generic looking show amidst a sea of them.

Vince McMahon appears first, to announce the "host and star" of the show: his son Shane McMahon. Could there be a crappier way to start this broadcast than with sickening nepotism? Shane struts out looking every bit the spoilt brat rich kid, flanked by two hot women no less. He is a ladies' man, you see. As anyone who read *The Raw Files 1998* will be aware, Shane is a terrible commentator. He shows his idiocy right away by trying to talk without putting his headset on, then starts yelling garbled nonsense during Edge's entrance. Oh, this is going to be hard work.

Edge vs. Jeff Jarrett
At least we are starting with what should be a good match on paper. Jarrett is currently going through a phase of being determined to have good matches with everyone, whereas Edge is eager to make up for his disastrous debut a few months back when he accidentally broke Jose Estrada's neck. "Going down town, bang, bang, bang," yells Shane as Edge hits a spear and rams Jarrett into the mat. He commentates like an ADHD kid who has only consumed sugar and coffee for a week straight. He bounces back-and-forth between calls, first yelling at the action and then getting distracted by his women. The camera spends a lot of time on him, which is marvellous. Shane talks over JR then tries to be him, calling every single move and offering his decidedly non-insightful opinion on everything. "Going down town," he squawks again, then proceeds to seek JR's approval on every call, before asking, "How does that feel?" after every move. I don't believe it, but he is actually worse than Michael Cole! Genuinely. The match doesn't have a chance because it is enveloped by Shane's ego. If anyone cares, Edge picks up the win after Tennessee Lee accidentally trips Jarrett. I am furious with Shane, because he absolutely ruined what could have been a good match. And he is going to be commentating on *everything* on this show. Kill me now.
Final Rating: *

Mario Lopez, formerly Slater on *Saved By The Bell*, is sat in the crowd. The WWF sure are breaking out the big guns for this debut edition of *HeAT*!

Promo Time: Triple H and X-Pac
Once the catchphrases are out of the way, Jerry Lawler conducts an interview with the DX pair. He asks them about being forced to wrestle each other tomorrow night on *RAW* in a match to determine the new number one contender for the Intercontinental Title. They are not overly worried about the prospect. Trips points out that Vince has never liked DX from the start, but that they are the most "titillating" part of "this" show each week. This show,

Hunter? Trips forces some skanks in the crowd to flash their (censored) tits under mass peer-pressure, causing Shane to get overly excited. He jumps up and down on his chair like a hyperactive child, and throws some crotch chops. "Whoo! Bang it Triple H!" SHUT UP SHANE! This was utterly pointless.

We get footage from a segment called *Droz's World* where Droz talks about throwing up on Mark Henry during a training match, which freaked out the match's referee Tom Prichard. With killer deep vignettes like this, it remains a mystery that the man delightfully known as "Puke" didn't get over.

Droz & The Headbangers vs. Kaientai
This is slap bang in the middle of the infamous "choppy choppy your pee-pee" angle involving Val Venis and Kaientai. Val has just been caught in the shower with Yamaguchi-san's wife, and he turns up in the aisle before this starts to rub it in. He spends the match gyrating up against Mrs. Yamaguchi, who JR calls "a carnivore". That's a curious thing to say. Kaientai bring their usual double and triple teaming finesse to the dance, but their opponents are hardly the right guys to keep up with them. To their credit, they do at least try. Shane is still talking constantly throughout, so much so that Jerry Lawler has now been removed from the announce team because he couldn't get a word in edgeways. Back to the match and Kaientai isolate Thrasher, but Droz gets an apathetic hot tag and things break down with all six guys in the ring. Droz hits a sit-out powerbomb on Men's Teiho for the win, and no one cares. Now to the real purpose of this match: furthering the Val Venis angle. He struts down to the ring for a confrontation with the Japanese contingent, but they just walk away without uttering a word to him. Val turns his attentions to Mario Lopez's *Pacific Blue* co-star Amy Hunter-Cornelius, and shoves Lopez down in his seat when he tells him to leave her alone. Lopez loses his temper and jumps the barricade, then takes out Val with a double leg before getting carted away by security. Wow, talk about random and pointless celebrity cameos!
Final Rating: *¼

Next, the return of the WWF's stock-music panpipes track! Last seen in a WWF Home Video release during highlights of the Triple H vs. The Rock ladder match from *SummerSlam*! Wow. Actually, *SummerSlam* is after this so I guess this appearance in the origin! It plays over the top of a Sable/Vince video detailing the former's return to the WWF... after a week "retired".

WWF European Championship
D'Lo Brown (c) vs. Ken Shamrock
This is kept short, and Mark Henry interferes when he gets the opportunity, allowing D'Lo to take control of the bout. Almost immediately Dan Severn and Steve Blackman come out for a closer look, meaning there are more wrestlers on the outside than in the ring. D'Lo methodically chops away at Shamrock but gets caught with a desperation belly-to-belly and both men are down. "What's going on with the ref?" asks Shane for no apparent reason other than to hear his own voice. D'Lo ends up on the outside after a Shamrock rana where he comes face-to-face with Severn, the man who caused him to have to wear the chest-protector he has been sporting recently. Severn jumps in the ring after him and causes the DQ, which infuriates the perma-angry Shamrock. Post match he beats the shit out of the ring steps with a steel chair. Because he is nuts. Almost nothing happened in the ring here. Again, the match was only there to further the angles involving the guys in it.
Final Rating: ½*

More *Pacific Blue* crossover next (*HeAT* is the lead-in for the show on the *USA Network*) as series star Shanna Moaker interviews Bart Gunn backstage, discussing his recent shock demolition of Steve Williams in the *Brawl For All*. Bart says he respects 'Dr. Death' but he caught him with a good left. Moaker asks Gunn to show him some moves and snuggles up to him on a couch. Way to go, Bart!

Kane & Mankind vs. The Rock & Owen Hart

Here is your main event then: an all-heel tag match! Booking geniuses, I tell you. At least there is some top talent involved, so hopefully they will overcome the limitations that have been imposed on them by the odd matchmaking. There is a purpose to the nonsense if that's any consolation, as the winner gets a title shot against tag champions Steve Austin and The Undertaker tomorrow night on *RAW*. Well, in theory at least. Kane and Mankind target Rock early on, making the Nation duo de facto babyfaces for the time being. The crowd is still reluctant to cheer too vociferously for Rock so content themselves with chanting "nugget" at Owen. Kane hits a flying clothesline as we go to commercial and Shane once again inquires as to how it feels. He is still talking as the ads kick in, and when we return he is yammering the split second we start back, directly reminding everyone who he is and that he is the host and star of the show. He has some serious ego problems. His commentary hasn't improved since Lawler left either, and he continues to sound like a parody of a wrestling announcer, with JR audibly irked by his belligerence. Back to the match and Owen tries to work heat on Kane but doesn't have much success. Kane hits a chokeslam, prompting further queries from Shane regarding the magnitude of the blow: "How's your back, Owen?" Things break down on the outside, but Owen beats the ref's count and wins the match for his team. This was rotten.

Final Rating: *

Backstage, Michael Cole simply has to make an appearance to further darken my mood. He questions why Steve Austin threw The Undertaker a beer on *RAW*, and Austin says he looked thirsty, then points out that the two are no closer now as tag champions than they were before. Then following Shane desperately trying to get in the last word, we are done.

THE HEAT RECAP:

Most Entertaining: Jim Ross. Nobody was good tonight, except JR. He deserves all the credit in the world for putting up with Shane.

Least Entertaining: Shane McMahon. After reading the above, I shouldn't need to explain why.

Shane McMahon Sound Effect of the Night: "Bang! Bang! Bang!"

Match of the Night: I can't award one in good faith.

Summary: Awful. The inaugural episode of *Sunday Night HeAT* was a complete and utter disaster. The wrestling was rushed, illogically booked or engulfed by angles, and the segments were dire. The worst of all though was of course Shane McMahon, who turned a drab broadcast into an unbearable one. I have always considered Michael Cole to be the worst commentator of all time, and make no mistake he is right up there, but Shane McMahon delved to new levels of atrocious tonight. And the worst thing? There is much more of the same to

come from him. Perhaps this book was a bad idea!
Verdict: 17

08.09.98 by James Dixon
Venue: San Diego, CA
Taped: 07.28.98
TV Rating: 4.2

Promo Time: Mankind
"Kaboom!" bellows out imbecilic host (and star of the show) Shane McMahon as Kane makes his entrance alongside Mankind. "Fire! Fire! Fire! Fire! Fire!" he screams, like a complete moron, when Kane does his ringpost gimmick. As ever, Mick Foley can't resist talking about Christmas, mentioning a recent family vacation to Christmas Village with his daughter Noelle. He tells a nice story, but one that significantly lessens his heel dastardly-ness. He moves on to the Undertaker and rips into him for trying to cripple him at *King of the Ring*, then rags on the crowd for not giving him a standing ovation after that bout. He says because of that he will never wrestle again for the fans, and that his career won't end in a blaze of glory but rather he will just become so broken down that he will have to stop, and no one will care. This is very introspective, self-effacing and tragic. It's a babyface promo, truth be told, though despite the sentiment, it is delivered with such passion that it works. Solid stuff from Mick on the mic, as always.

Vader vs. Mark Henry
Pie-facing starts us off, then Mark Henry military presses Vader right off the bat. Unreal strength. "He's out of control," offers Shane, a sentence that he is either trying to get over as a catchphrase, or he is just so goddamn stupid that he doesn't realise he says it every match. Henry starts yelling and Shane responds that, "I'm feeling your dogs." He is so hip and down with the street slang. The match takes place mostly in slow motion, with a spot on the outside where Henry sends Vader into the steps looking especially awful. At least we get blood, with Vader busting the rookie with shots to the mouth. It doesn't slow him much, and Henry smashes Vader with four big splashes and leaves him for dead. Shane squeals his approval, but the referee doesn't like the excessive violence so disqualifies Henry for refusing to go for the pin. Horrible decision, frankly. I hate seeing Vader wasted like this, but it did make Henry look brutal.
Final Rating: *

The Headbangers vs. Southern Justice
I am not sure what to make of this continued union betwixt Droz and the Headbangers, with the former accompanying the metal-heads once again. I remember a match that these two teams had at *Badd Blood* last October and it was shockingly bad. And that was before the Godwinns became a pair of generic tubby blokes in bad suits. JR has developed a new technique for dealing with Shane; he starts a sentence, ignores Shane completely when he talks over him, and then continues what he was saying. It's hilarious, and just sounds like Shane is ranting to himself like a gibbering baboon. "This match is just out of control," reckons Shane as things break down. Droz and Jeff Jarrett get themselves involved and that is another DQ. At least it's over.
Final Rating: ¼*

Video Control brings us a hype video for the Oddities, which Shane wrongly claims is for the Insane Clown Posse.

TAKA Michinoku vs. X-Pac
I am going to try and ignore Shane and watch these two supremely talented athletes go at it. It's easier said than

done, as he gets overly excited about the appearance of John Wayne Bobbitt on tomorrow night's *RAW* rather than calling the bout. They work this at a decent pace, as you would expect, with both utilising kicks. Unfortunately it is super-brief, with Pac picking up the win after less than three minutes with the X-Factor. Kaientai jump Pac after the bell, but DX run in and take them out, showing a unity that has been missing in recent weeks. Yamaguchi escapes and mockingly dances on the ramp, but Chyna decks him from behind and DX do some posing and mooning. Three guesses what Shane thinks they are? That's right, "Out of control."
Final Rating: *¾

Highlights from *Pacific Blue* next which features Triple H. JR quips that he is one of few wrestlers to appear on the big screen (though technically big screen would be a movie, but okay...) who hasn't embarrassed himself. A sly dig at Hulk Hogan, Roddy Piper and Jesse Ventura for sure, but what about WWF's favourite legend Andre the Giant? His starring role as Fezzik in *The Princess Bride* was superb.

Bradshaw vs. Dustin Runnels

These two have a surprisingly large amount of TV matches in 1998, and the majority of them suck. This one is especially bad because Dustin is doing his evangelist gimmick, which is far worse than his later Black Rain or Seven guises away from the WWF. Thankfully Bradshaw is in no mood to dick around and he smashes through Runnels quickly, finishing him with the always delightful Clothesline From Hell. Dustin seeks solace in prayer after the bout.
Final Rating: ½*

This week on *Droz's World* we get to hear about his crappy tattoos.

Droz vs. Jeff Jarrett

"The Droz, he's out of control." No prizes for guessing who said that. I honestly, genuinely despise Shane McMahon behind the announce desk. Another example of his overbearing idiocy follows seconds later when JR hypes the upcoming Mankind vs. Undertaker match tonight, and all Shane can offer is, "Fight! Fight! Fight! Fight! Fight!" Jarrett once again finds himself in a position where he is forced to work twice as hard as usual to get a decent match out of an inferior worker, and as usual he bumps his ass off for his opponent. Southern Justice show up mere seconds into the bout, and Jarrett uses the distraction of their appearance to take over. The "heat" lasts all of ten seconds before Droz fights back, but Jarrett cuts him right off with a slow DDT. "Droz will never be a finesse wrestler," offers Ross, which is a shoot. Jarrett utilises a sleeper hold so he can call the remainder of the match to the inexperienced Droz, and then the Headbangers show up as Droz hits a flying clothesline. They run a double down after a collision in the centre of the ring, and Tennessee Lee throws a cowboy boot in for Jarrett, but Droz sees it first and uses it to score the win. Yeah, babyfaces shouldn't be winning like that. Once again Jarrett has lost thanks to Lee, and his losing streak continues. Lee defends himself after the match and says that Jarrett has a problem, suggesting Southern Justice are going to beat him up. Naturally this being the WWF in the Attitude Era, things don't pan out that way. Instead they deck Lee, and a triple team signals the end of their time together.
Final Rating: *¼

Mankind vs. The Undertaker

There is literally a minute left on this show, so this isn't happening. Mankind stands on the apron and says he is going to tear the Undertaker apart, but

then Kane from the ring shoves him off the apron and through a table. He follows up by decking Paul Bearer with a punch, then wipes out Mankind with steel steps. A Tombstone on the floor puts an exclamation point on things as confusion abounds. Then Kane unmasks and reveals himself to be the Undertaker, and suddenly it all makes sense. Erm, sort of. How did he get the gear? Did Kane lend it to him? I am not amused that we don't get the promised match, but at least the angle was pretty good.
Final Rating: N/R

THE HEAT RECAP:

Most Entertaining: Mankind. Decent promo at the start and some nice bumps at the end.

Least Entertaining: Shane McMahon. He was out of control.

Shane McMahon Sound Effect of the Night: "Kaboom!"

Match of the Night: TAKA Michinoku vs. X-Pac. Criminally short, but easily the best match.

Summary: Well it was better than last week's fiasco, but still a tough watch. The WWF would do well to reduce the amount of matches and give everything a little more time, not to mention more clean finishes, but that is unfortunately par for the course in 1998 across the board. HeAT struggles more than RAW because it also has the immense burden of Shane McMahon dragging the decent stuff down by completely distracting the viewer with his insistence on talking nonsense non-stop for every second of the broadcast. Let's hope these first two weeks are simply teething problems.
Verdict: 27

08.16.98 by James Dixon
Venue: Omaha, NE
Taped: 08.10.98
TV Rating: 3.4

You might think I have been unduly harsh on this show the past two weeks, given its status as a definite secondary show with an hour run time. But, that never stopped *RAW* in its early years. In 1993 *RAW* was not the flagship show, despite what history might state. Yet, it managed to be entertaining on a weekly basis and feature some truly great matches. The problem with *HeAT* is the booking, with too many matches, too much Shane McMahon and nothing pertinent happening. Maybe that will all change this week...

WWF Tag Team Championship
Kane & Mankind (c) vs. LOD 2000
In keeping with those aforementioned early *RAW* shows, we open with a main event. Sadly, LOD 2000 is Animal and Droz, with Hawk having "problems". Droz isn't even in his "Puke" attire yet, just his generic flannel pants. "HAVING A BLAST?" asks Shane obnoxiously to Jim Ross, randomly. This show is all about him you see, the match doesn't matter. As long as Shane gets his mug on the box, *HeAT* is a success. As ever, JR looks entirely put out by it all. The match is heatless, though Droz does bleed hardway from something or other. Animal uses a chair and the referee turns a blind eye, but it doesn't help much. Kane quickly finishes him off with the Tombstone and that is all she wrote. "BOOOOOOM!" bellow Shane. It's one of his better calls in the entire match.
Final Rating: ¾*

Promo Time: Jacqueline
Jackie recently debuted and lost courtesy of Sable interference. She calls out the balloon-chested one using rhyme, with her appearance prompting a "Schwing!" call from Shane. Yes, it's a

Wayne's World reference, and yes it was dated even then, coming six years after the movie's release. At least he is keeping up the family tradition of being on the very pulse of modern pop culture. Not! See, I can do it too... Sable squawks, then calls Jackie a cheap hooker. Ah, good old Attitude. Sable says she can beat Jackie at anything and then walks off. Another killer promo from the very definition of dumb blonde stereotype.

Edge vs. Brian Christopher

Edge is still dark and brooding whereas Christopher is not yet "Sexay", thus neither man is over. Christopher's hot dogging gets him planted with an electric chair drop, which Shane pops bigger than anyone. Meanwhile in the crowd, Dustin Runnels wanders around with inspirational placards. Edge is the aggressor until Scott Taylor helps out, his distraction allowing Christopher to hit his always-nasty slingshot powerbomb on the outside. He has it won with a top rope bulldog, but instead of pinning he walks around the ring, struts and hugs Taylor. He really is booked as the dumbest motherfucker on the planet. Edge catches Christopher off the top with a spinebuster and hits a naff spear, not a patch on later years, but Christopher counters back with what will become known as The Stroke. Tennessee Jam finds nothing but ring, and Edge finishes with the Downward Spiral. Probably the best match in the history of *HeAT* so far...
Final Rating: **

Bart Gunn vs. Vader

Yep, Vader is still around. Just about. Godfather is at ringside for this as he has Bart in the *Brawl For All* on *RAW* tomorrow. "He's no friend of mine," grumbles JR of Gunn, bitterly. Why would any fighter take a match the day before a big fight? The story is built around the knockout power in Bart's left hand, which I guess he must have forgot that he possessed in his five year WWF career prior to this. Bart is booked to look like Vader's equal, which is quite a thing to witness. He doesn't get to go over though, because he is attacked at ringside by Godfather leaded to a DQ. Vader splashes him after the fact to add injury to, well, injury. This was interesting actually, just seeing Bart being treated *almost* like a star. However, the highlight of the match was JR chastising Shane for smoking Godfather's cigar: "Your daddy wouldn't approve of you smoking that cigarette, I just want to let you know that," he admonishes. Those winking insider comments, you can't beat 'em. For those unaware, Vince abhors smoking.
Final Rating: *½

Gangrel vs. Scott Taylor

Busy night for the future Scotty 2 Hotty. "I don't know what he's doing JR," observes Shane, and for the first time in three weeks I agree with him. The comment comes because Gangrel has apparently decided that he is a lucha star, and throws baffling rolls in between his spots like... well, nothing I have seen. It is very strange. This is brief, because we have a main event interview to get to imminently, with Gangrel over via the Impaler.
Final Rating: SQUASH (Not rated)

Promo Time: Tiger Ali Singh

Oh just shoot me. The foreign guy hates Americans, so he challenges anyone from the crowd to eat a live worm. Marty Wright accepts and the Boogeyman is born.*

* Note, this was not the actual origin of the Boogeyman

Triple H & X-Pac vs. Southern Justice

Shane, who Hunter with hilarious retrospective irony calls, "the heir apparent to the WWF throne", sings

along with Hunter's pre-match spiel, complete with requisite "boom" exclamation to round it off. Did I mention that he is annoying? To my disappointment, no reference is made to Hunter and HOG's storied, pig shit-filled past. Southern Justice clobber away for a minute or so before Pac tags in and wipes out PIG's face with a spinning kick. Holy hell! I have genuinely seen less brutal knockout kicks in UFC. Things spill outside, with Justice beating on Hunter, allowing their running buddy and Pac's *SummerSlam* opponent to come in and kick Pac in the nads. That's a DQ, naturally. By the numbers stuff, but that kick was ridiculous.
Final Rating: ½*

Promo Time: The Undertaker

By the time Taker gets the mic, there are only two minutes left on the show. Helluva main event. Taker speaks directly into the camera, which is a rare sight in the WWF. That is another of Vince's infamously nutty pet peeve idioms. Steve Austin listens backstage to Taker saying how he has pissed him off. He doesn't need to hear any more and heads out. The crowd is surprisingly muted for this. Mind you, they had just sat through a *Shotgun* taping featuring the Harris twins and the Headbangers, not to mention a full episode of *RAW*, with not a decent match in sight. It's hard to blame them. Kane appears on the stage leaving Austin trapped on the ramp between the Brothers of Destruction, as we go off the air.

THE HEAT RECAP:

Most Entertaining: X-Pac. Anyone who kicks Phineas Godwinn in the face is okay with me.

Least Entertaining: Sable. That voice! Picture an argument between her and hubby Brock Lesnar. Imagine those two screeching voices at full pitch. No wonder they live on a farm, far away from everyone else.

Shane McMahon Sound Effect of the Night: "Boom!"

Match of the Night: Edge vs. Brian Christopher. It actually bordered on "decent".

Summary: Far too rushed again. A show full of criminally short matches, teases or angles that didn't deliver and unbearable performers like Sable, Tiger and Shane. Filming this show at the end of a long taping was a terrible idea from the WWF, because the crowd was just dead and the wrestlers clearly wanted to be anywhere else. With each week I regret more and more the decision to do this book.
Verdict: 17

08.23.98 by James Dixon
Venue: Des Moines, IA
Taped: 08.11.98
TV Rating: 3.6

Hosted, as ever, by Jim Ross, Shane McMahon and some random chick that Shane has brought with him. She is actually listed on the graphic as "friend". This was filmed nearly two weeks ago prior to *RAW* rather than after it, so at least the crowd should be relatively hot.

The Oddities vs. Southern Justice

What's that famous JR phrase again? "Bowling shoe ugly". That should about sum this up, I suspect. Before we get underway, The Rock comes out to his music, places a ladder on the stage, gets announced by Tony Chimmel, and then leaves. Okay, random interlude of the day! Kurrgan squaring off with Dennis Knight is way better than you would reasonably expect. When Golga comes in, it causes my mind to wander and contemplate the spectacle that

would be Earthquake vs. Phineas Godwinn. It's like one of those wrestling general knowledge questions: when did [insert name] and [insert name] wrestle? Here! In this match! If only Typhoon were here. Southern Justice try and build heat on Golga, but he is nearly four hundred pounds so, y'know. Shane thinks Mark Canterbury is 340lbs. I guess he sees the wrestling world through his father's eyes. Standard cheap finish here, with Luna's interference causing a DQ. Jeff Jarrett heads down to even the score and threatens to cut Luna's hair, though I am not sure what that would achieve. She uses to shave half of her head bald anyway. Giant Silva lumbers in to deliver a massive chokeslam and the crowd go nuts. I like the Oddities, I really do. Christ, that wasn't even too bad. Actually, it was fairly enjoyable! I eat my words!
Final Rating: **

WWF European Championship
D'Lo Brown (c) vs. Animal

Drunk Hawk, one of my least acceptable guilty pleasures, has found his way to ringside. He jumps in the ring to give Animal support, but his partner doesn't want it. "Shape up punk, or you're gonna be shipped out," says Shane, perhaps conveying a message from his dad. Mark Henry gets involved and splashes Hawk on the outside, then he and D'Lo do a number on Animal. Droz makes the save, and we don't get a match here.
Final Rating: N/R

A montage of the best moments in the *Brawl For All* follows, highlighting the knockouts in particular. I bet Jim Ross just loves seeing constant replays of Steve Williams getting floored. This makes the tournament look really exciting. You know, even though it was utterly ludicrous, it *was* fun to watch. Wow, three guilty pleasures in one night. I am in hog's heaven.

The Headbangers
vs. Dan Severn & Owen Hart

This is something of a contrast in ideologies. Severn is another guy I enjoy and feel was criminally underused. That guy could have been a killer heel. Think Harvey Keitel as Winston Wolfe, that sort of demeanour. Mosh works over Severn while canned heat plays over the top, suggesting the fans in the building were less than enamoured by this one. Ross and Shane feel the same way and run through the upcoming USA Network schedule. Why is the heel Severn, the biggest guy in the match no less, taking the heat here? Owen blind tags in to arrest the ennui, but he is not a miracle worker. This is still the Headbangers, after all. An utterly by-the-numbers tag affair until Owen finishes things with a dragon sleeper. Among the most tedious Owen matches you will see.
Final Rating: DUD

Promo Time: The Rock

Rock opts for the cheap heat route and insults the crowd before getting to the meat of his promo: answering Triple H's challenge to a ladder match at *SummerSlam*. Though, Rock's acceptance is hardly a revelation given his earlier ladder histrionics. Or the fact he has a ladder in the ring whilst he is talking. He uses it as a prop, climbing the people's ladder and threatening to kick Hunter's ass. Very, very generic promo from the master.

The WWF run an advert for a line of Jakks figures called Slammers 2. The six figures available? The Patriot (not seen since Fall 1997), Dude Love (put out to pasture in May), Shawn Michaels ("retired" after *WrestleMania XIV)*, Kane, Taka Michinoku and Brian Pillman (died October 1997). I can understand when they release video

TAKA Michinoku vs. Scorpio

Hello, what potential hidden delight is this? Sadly this is not the four star mini-classic it could be, rather a quickie TV match at half speed. Taka still breaks out an Asai moonsault and takes some big bumps, but it is nothing out of the ordinary. Actually, there is a fairly naff bit where Scorp signals for the 450, only to pick Taka up and hit another move on the opposite side of the ring. He does so because Mrs. Yamaguchi has a planned spot that calls for her to stand on the apron and distract the ref, and he doesn't trust her to move into position. I understand his reasoning, but it looks very poor. The distraction leads to a Michinoku Driver ("Mickey-No-Coo Driver" if you are Shane) and Taka wins. If this had taken place in 2015, people would be chanting "Yes!" in support of Scorpio to try and change the course of his future.

Final Rating: *¾

Apparent *HeAT* regular, Mario Lopez, puts over the WWF in a brief VT. We never did get that Val Venis vs. Slater match. Strange that another member of the *Saved By The Bell* crew, Screech, did get involved (ish) in wrestling.

A five minute video package follows, covering the Steve Austin and Undertaker summer-long feud, that climaxes next week at *SummerSlam*. The "highway to hell" build up was great for this match, though Shane thinks the part that stood out the most was Austin driving a hearse into the arena and "shocking the world". Once again, he sees the wrestling world through his papa's eyes.

Jeff Jarrett vs. Droz

The lengthy highlight video means we only have around two minutes of airtime left for the main event, which is billed as Droz's chance for revenge. Jarrett cut his hair, you see, though most would agree he did him a favour. The couple of minutes they get are what they are, but the story is the appearance of X-Pac (dressed like a farmer's daughter clad in denim overalls), who takes a lock of Jarrett's hair. Droz tries to stick it on his head as we go off the air.

Final Rating: N/R

THE HEAT RECAP:

Most Entertaining: The Oddities. You heard me right, I didn't stutter!

Least Entertaining: The Headbangers.

Shane McMahon Sound Effect of the Night: "Woaaaaooooaaaahhoo, Booooom!"

Match of the Night: The Oddities vs. Southern Justice. Yes, I genuinely enjoyed this more than Taka vs. Scorpio.

Summary: Not a bad episode this week in places, and it certainly went by quickly. I find that when the show has more short matches it goes slowly, but less bouts given slightly longer has a much better flow. I was genuinely surprise by the opening match. I was expecting drizzles and I got a rainbow. It's all relative of course, but it is nice when a match doesn't suck to the levels you expect it will, especially on a secondary show that only half as many people watch compared to *RAW*. The tapings taking place prior to *RAW* helps a great deal, and Shane appears to have toned down his hyperactive act a little, whether intentionally or otherwise. He is not good, no no no, but he is a lot more bearable than in the first two weeks. For that alone, I would consider this a mild success.

Verdict: 31

08.30.98 by James Dixon
Venue: New York, NY
Taped: 08.30.98
TV Rating: 3.2

Ah ha! Goodbye burned out crowd, hello Madison Square Garden! This is the first episode of the show to be aired directly prior to a pay-per-view, coming right before the excellent *SummerSlam '98*. I am hoping for a jacked audience and a host of workers eager to make an impression in the world's most famous arena. We open with Shawn Michaels heading out to join Jim Ross and Shane McMahon on commentary, though no sign of Shane's "friend" today.

LOD 2000 vs. Too Much
Hawk remains impaired and is replaced by Droz, but that doesn't stop him heading out wearing his helmet and making a nuisance of himself. "Does anyone know what his problem is?" asks Shawn. I would hazard a guess that you probably have a better idea than most, Mr. Michaels. Hawk forces his way into the match and takes up a spot on the apron, and Droz just vanishes into thin air. A decade ago, this match is a sub-two minute squash with zero selling, but we are in a different time. Jim Ross even notes as much. Remarkably, Animal takes the heat and he sells for the two guys half his size. He remembers who he is and decks both, but refuses to tag the wasted Hawk. Animal looks to have the job done, but that zany drunkard climbs the ropes for the Doomsday Device facing the wrong way, accidentally nails Animal, and causes him to get pinned. Too Much beat the Road Warriors in the Garden. Wow.
Final Rating: *

Backstage, Steve Austin is wandering around with a sledgehammer, waiting for the arrival of the Undertaker and Kane. This was long before Triple H made the oversized phallus his weapon of choice.

Promo Time: Sable
Shawn Michaels takes to the ring and introduces Sable. Talk about two voices that could curdle milk. Shawn makes jokes about Sable's big tits, and she appreciates the attention. Shawn asks who her partner is tonight in her mixed tag match on the pay-per-view, but she won't reveal her hand. Instead she tells us who it isn't, which is the Oddities. "Their dance card is full tonight," she says, before segueing awkwardly into asking Shawn to dance sexily for her. He doesn't need asking twice. What a redundant segment. Any time Sable talks is an automatic switch off of course.

Dustin Runnels vs. Gangrel
The Preacher vs. The Vampire. It might be the Attitude Era, but it is still a giant cartoon. I am amused by Gangrel's selling of his blood drinking gimmick. He drinks it pre-match as ever, then develops a look of sheer orgasmic pleasure as if the blood just got him hard. It's silly, but it does make sense for the character. "That shirt is a little bit gothic in my view," says Jim Ross. Well, yeah! Unfortunately Gangrel is all sizzle and little steak, with his entrance the best part of the match. They just go through the motions, with the crowd amusing themselves in other ways. Gangrel finishes with the DDT in a quick, inoffensive but entirely unmemorable encounter. This existed purely to fill time.
Final Rating: ¾*

Meanwhile, they are still replaying the Val Venis/Mario Lopez segment from a few weeks ago as nauseum. They really love these pointless celebrity cameos. What a waste of time though, because it's not like it ever led to a match between them. Not that I would want to see that of course!

Backstage, Michael Cole interviews Vince McMahon. He gets a hail of abuse from the Garden. Vince is worried about Austin and his sledgehammer, concerned that his main event is in jeopardy. He promises to do something about it.

In the ring, Jeff Jarrett and Southern Justice jump The Fink and shave his head and moustache. "Not the gimmick! Not the gimmick!" yells Michaels at the prospect of Finkel losing his trademark lip slug. Nobody was off limits to be involved in angles in the Attitude Era. Silly but fine as a way to hype the hair versus hair match tonight between Jarrett and X-Pac.

DOA vs. Bradshaw & Vader

Is there a more disappointment-inducing sound in all of wrestling than the opening strains of DOA's music? As soon as you hear it you know you are in for five minutes of tedium. It's time that you can never get back. Their opponents are an odd couple pairing, though one that could have worked had the WWF been interested in treating them seriously. They could have had some decent matches as well, a WWF version of Vader and Stan Hansen. Sadly, poor Vader's stock has dropped to depths hitherto unseen, a decision I still can't quite fathom. The main event scene was so thin in 1998 beyond Austin, Taker and Kane in various combinations over and over, and Vader always had good matches with Austin. He would have been a decent opponent for a quick one-PPV feud, or indeed a long program. Instead, he gets rolled up by one of the worthless DOA twins and pinned. What a joke. This company made money despite itself. Bradshaw is pissed off about the defeat, so he and Vader trade punches and brawl a bit to set up a program that goes nowhere.

Final Rating: ½*

Backstage, Vince and his Stooges confront Austin and try to stop him from hitting anyone with his hammer. It goes about as well for them as expected.

Michael Hayes does the world's corniest introduction to the "highway to hell" video that they have been running for months. They were very proud of this one. Hey, it's a good video, but after seeing it every week for the past month's worth of TV it starts getting a little stale.

Another *SummerSlam* video follows, this one pushing the Triple H versus Rock ladder match. Again, it is a decent enough hype tool, but nothing new.

And then a truncated version of the "highway to hell" video airs again! Come on now!

Rock hits the ring with the Nation for a promo and manages to get a single sentence out before DX head down for a brawl. It lasts about twenty seconds, then we cut backstage to Steve Austin watching a hearse arrive. He smashes it to pieces with his hammer, but there is no sign of Taker or Kane. Not satisfied, he finds a well-placed forklift truck and continues his vehicular assault as we go off the air.

THE HEAT RECAP:

Most Entertaining: Gangrel. For the pure unadulterated pleasure he gets from performing his own gimmick.

Least Entertaining: DOA.

Shane McMahon Sound Effect of the Night: "Big Bombs! BOOM!"

Match of the Night: LOD 2000 vs. Too Much. One snowflake, yet it wins easily.

Summary: It's a hype show and little else. Some of it was fine and did the job of promoting *SummerSlam* well, the rest was largely rushed filler. I didn't much care for the treatment of legendary industry figures Vader and the Legion of Doom, but that's sadly par for the course around this time. Not a show to go out of your way to see, but worth sticking on first if you are planning to re-watch *SummerSlam '98* again.
Verdict: 22

09.06.98 by Arnold Furious
Venue: New Haven, CT
Taped: 08.31.98
TV Rating: 3.2

The good thing about us covering *Sunday Night Heat* is that it's a show I barely watched first time around, so almost all of this is going to be new to me. All of 1998's *Raw* shows have come washing back like fond memories, but *Heat* will be a trip into the same time, the same place and all new entertainment. I'm expecting slightly more wrestling than *Raw* showcases and hoping for bouts featuring the better workers of the era in a less pressure-filled environment. What I'll probably get is DOA matches. And lots of them. I realise *Heat* was treated as a big deal to begin with so the initial shows might be loaded with big names, which is unfortunate as that tends to eliminate the in-ring that I'm hoping to see.

We're in New Haven, Connecticut. Hosts are Jim Ross and Shane McMahon. The absolute worst thing about reviewing this show is that it'll involve listening to Shane McMahon talk, almost non-stop, for an hour at a time. At least here he lets JR handle the play-by-play. As James discovered, that isn't always the case.

Gangrel vs. Dick Togo
Dropping into *Heat* can be a bit confusing, time-line wise, as the storylines don't jump out quite so easily. This is about a month after Gangrel's debut. He's had issues with Edge already ("this rivalry is heating up," chimes Shane). Early contributions from Shane include calling *Blade* "awesome" and insisting "pop's" masterplan is a "doozy". I can imagine seeing Shane in a bar around this time and leaving because he's the loud, obnoxious guy who thinks he knows everything and his opinion is always EXTREME. Everything is "awesome" or it sucks. I can't abide him. Togo is on fire and throws in a load of cool spots before Gangrel gets his shit in. Togo does a glorious little no-selling bit, which is typically Japanese and reminds me of modern day Japanese warrior Tomohiro Ishii. Gangrel beats him back down and finishes with the Impaler. Shane barely stops talking about his dad to shout "OH YEAH, OH YEAH," at a replay of the finish. Thanks for that, Shane.
Final Rating: *¼

Video Control gives us footage of Marc Mero awarding Jacqueline with a trophy because "that stupid Sable" broke the other one. This is followed by a US Open spoof where the Undertaker battles DX in a five-on-one tennis brawl. This is part of the WWF's general anger with being replaced by tennis on Mondays by the USA Network. It's a terrific little ad break though, and included Kane as the line judge calling a Billy Gunn serve as "in", despite it clearing the stand.

Ken Shamrock vs. Bradshaw
If *Raw*'s standard match run-time is three minutes, then *Heat*'s, by virtue of being a shorter show, is about two. Two minutes isn't enough to tell a story, so Shamrock and Bradshaw just take it in turns to get their spots in. Shane

actually makes a competent point by suggesting Bradshaw's size advantage means nothing because Shamrock can ankle lock anyone. It makes no difference here because Vader runs in for the DQ after, - ta-da - two minutes. Shamrock threatens to kill the ref after he calls it a victory for Bradshaw on DQ, which it is. Learn the rules, Kenny.
Final Rating: ¾*

Road Dogg vs. Dennis Knight

Billy gets upset that Road Dogg doesn't name-drop him during the introductions. "But Billy isn't wrestling tonight". He eventually does it anyway, thus completing the best part of the match. Dennis tries to not ruin the entire bout with his usual stinkiness and takes a few big bumps. Unfortunately they then decide to run heat. Heat on *Heat*. This being Dennis Knight, it's really dull. Luckily the match is also only two minutes long so eventually the heat has to end, which it does when Jeff Jarrett runs in for the DQ. Followed by X-Pac for the save. Shane decides to take over on play-by-play at this point, yelling everything that's happening in the ring. "YEAH RIGHT HANDS, BAM, BAM, BAM, BAM!" Urgh.
Final Rating: ¼*

The Undertaker & Kane vs. Animal & Droz

"YEAH, YOU HEAR THAT MUSIC? UNDERTAKER IS ON THE WAY". No shit, Shane. Take some downers, smoke some grass. Just mellow out. A stoned Shane McMahon would be just as irritating, but slightly less grating by virtue of reduced volume. I don't see the sense of burying Animal & Droz by having them in this match. No one gets the rub from working Taker & Kane, they just get squashed. Hawk joins via telephone to say he's checking into rehab tomorrow. Shane holds Giant Silva responsible because of a powerbomb last week. As if losing to Giant Silva is considered hitting rock bottom and leads to realising your alcoholism. As he was counting lights, he had a moment of clarity. Taker treating Animal like a jobber doesn't sit well with me. Especially as he decides to utilise his MMA leglock for the win, thus making him look like a total punk. I'm of the belief that Animal could have been a useful singles guy in 1999, and this kind of booking hurt him. Match was a squash, nothing more. Ironically this is the longest match on the card and yet the only one I've dubbed un-rateable on squash terms.
Final Rating: SQUASH

TAKA Michinoku vs. Edge

Oh wow, this could be good. If it gets longer than two minutes (Spoiler: it doesn't). "DING, DING, DING!" yells Shane to let us know we're underway. God, he's irritating. Kaientai on *Heat* is weird because they come out solo, despite always coming out in numbers on *Raw*. What makes *Heat* different? Like with the opener, both guys are eager to get their spots in and take it in turns to do so. It's improved by better bumps and TAKA being able to create a coherent little storyline. He thinks about the Michinoku Driver, but Edge counters into the Downward Spiral for the win. Match of the night. That's not saying much, but a longer match could have been really strong.
Final Rating: *½

Promo Time: Undertaker & Kane

Taker drags out Pat Patterson, Kane has Gerry Brisco. Taker demands to know Vince's masterplan or both his top Stooges are getting destroyed. McMahon is a no show so the Stooges take a beating and stereo chokeslams.

WWF European Championship
D'Lo Brown (c) vs. Val Venis

This is the main event and Brown's prestigious European title is on the line.

D'Lo hails from Warsaw, Poland this evening. Like most Poles he's working overseas. As if having a three-minute main event isn't enough of a challenge, there's also Dustin Runnels at ringside declaring "he is coming back" via sign. Like with the previous short back-and-forth bouts on the show, this is a short back-and-forth bout. Val gets planted into the exposed turnbuckle and D'Lo finishes with a German suplex. That's somewhat unexpected and JR claims it's Val's first loss. Technically Val lost a gauntlet match to Kaientai back in August and just last night was defeated by none other than D'Lo Brown. Although that was a DQ. So it's not so much his first loss, but certainly his first singles pinfall defeat. Post Match: Val rips off D'Lo's chest protector, hits a powerbomb and puts on the Chest Protector for the Money Shot. The match was okay, but really rushed.
Final Rating: *¼

Promo Time: Vince McMahon
He starts to repeat a few points regarding his masterplan, pointing out how easy he is to find to Taker and Kane. The crowd happily chant "Austin" and "asshole" to keep themselves amused. Vince offers an apology (for his "putrid pussies" remark), calling Taker and Kane the "single most destructive force in the WWF". Vince points out both Taker and Kane are now deserving of a title match and calls out Steve Austin to make it final. It's a lot of star power with very little happening. Vince finally gets around to booking Austin vs. Kane & Undertaker at the next PPV. "That isn't fair," moans JR as we go off the air. "That match will suck," moans me as I finish this paragraph.

THE HEAT RECAP:

Most Entertaining: TAKA Michinoku. Structured a tidy match with Edge.

Least Entertaining: Shane McMahon. Shouting stupid things with great frequency.

Quote of the Night: "He's a dandy alright" – JR's assessment of WWF owner Vince McMahon.

Match of the Night: Edge vs. TAKA Michinoku

Summary: This is my first exposure to *Heat*, and first impressions are that it comes off as a low-rent *Raw*. Yes, there is more wrestling on here than *Raw*, but some of the weaker Monday night shows were just lots of little, bad matches, exactly the same as this. You can't fit six matches into an hour and have them be worthwhile. All these matches are so forgettable I find it hard to recall them for the recap. Ideally in a forty-five minute show you need three matches at the most, and maybe one big angle. This is just too crowded. It's a big disappointment.
Verdict: 18

09.13.98 by Arnold Furious
Venue: Lowell, MA
Taped: 09.01.98
TV Rating: ??

Hosts are Jim Ross and Shane McMahon.

Ken Shamrock vs. Vader
Colour me excited to be getting this rematch from Shamrock's 1997 debut at *IYH: Cold Day in Hell*. Unfortunately Vader has been relegated to jobber status here, not even getting his own entrance. The idea, through *Heat* run-on booking, is that Shamrock was pissed off with Vader running in during his match with Bradshaw last week. Shamrock has changed since his WWF debut and spends most of this match hitting pro-wrestling spots rather than trying shoot-ish moves. Vader gets to

use his power and his heat segment is entertaining, even if the crowd are dead for it. Attitude crowds are supposed to be loud! Shamrock's spirited comeback is more sportz entertainment than MMA and Vader plants him with a powerbomb to block the rana. Shammy catches Vader coming off the top and counters into an ankle lock for the win. Smooth little contest but not a patch on their match from the previous year due to Vader's reduced role as glorified enhancement talent. Shamrock makes this more interesting by grabbing the microphone and pointing out that in eighteen months he's only had one title match, despite beating everyone bar Steve Austin. The challenge finally gets the crowd wet, but this was Kenny's last time as a main event threat before falling behind the likes of Mankind and Rock in the pecking order.
Final Rating: **¼

Video Control takes us to the set of *Pacific Blue* where Sable guest starred. She cuts a promo on Jacqueline from the set. No sign of Mario Lopez. A missed opportunity to make him guest star for a second time. We come back with Shane getting his makeup done "accidentally" on air. Oh the hilarity. "Anything can happen L-I-V-E," says Shane. Please go away.

Val Venis vs. Marc Mero

This is secondary to Dustin Runnels' "he is coming back" campaign, as he walks through the crowd holding up a sign. The actual match a is mere thirty seconds long before Jacqueline jumps in for the DQ. What's the point? Michael Cole arrives at ringside to ask Jacqueline about Sable's challenge to an Evening Gown Match, which she accepts. Meanwhile Dustin jumps in the ring to beat Venis down. Settle down, I said "Venis". Dustin's beat down is actually longer than the match. Nobody seems to care. I pretty much loathe this feud, and seeing it fall flat here is no surprise.
Final Rating: N/R

TAKA Michinoku vs. Gangrel

Poor TAKA, once again relegated to jobbing duty for "people of a Gothic lifestyle who happen to be heavyweights". WWF: the place where the light heavyweight championship is the title a jobber has. JR immediately points out how small he is. TAKA still dominates the match with his flying, because Gangrel's offence isn't much fun. TAKA makes it fun by taking all Gangrel's spots on his neck including a RELEASE TIGER SUPLEX. Oh the humanity! The commentators continue to make it about size and how tiny TAKA is. If you keep banging on about a person's weaknesses, as opposed to their strengths, that won't help that at all. Michinoku Driver is countered right into the Impaler, Gangrel's cool elevated DDT finish for the win. It would have been cooler if Edge hadn't done exactly the same thing with the Downward Spiral. Considering how brisk it was, the match was pretty good. Largely because of TAKA's bumping and the slick reversal on the finish.
Final Rating: *½

D'Lo Brown vs. Kane

This is right after The Rock saved D'Lo Brown on *Raw* - virtually turning himself babyface in the process - and D'Lo bailed, essentially ending the Nation of Domination for good. Obviously this is a mismatch and D'Lo, perhaps predictably, gets short thrift from Kane. He only sells for main eventers and plunder. Because Kane brings Taker down with him, D'Lo can't even run away. Mark Henry is in D'Lo's corner but he's not much help. D'Lo knows his role, probably after being told it by The Rock so many times, and basically just bounces around for Kane. The Rock gets sick of watching this business and

knocks Kane out with a chair. Despite this, Kane still no sells and would finish with a chokeslam only for Mark Henry to jump in for the DQ. Seeing as the post match just involves Taker and Kane mashing the Nation duo with finishers, I don't see why they didn't just put Kane over clean.
Final Rating: ½*

Lumberjack Match
Jeff Jarrett vs. X-Pac
Most of the lumberjacks are tag teams, including the Outlaws, the Headbangers, Too Much, DOA and Southern Justice. These two start hard and fast, throwing lumber (foot lumber from X-Pac) and countering. The lumberjack stipulation is paid lip service by one guy occasionally getting thrown to the floor, but they tend to stick to the in-ring. That's fine, because they're both good wrestlers. "Jeff does play a nasty tune with that guitar," points out Shane McMahon of Jarrett's "musical" ability, or lack thereof. "THIS MATCH IS AWESOME!" screams Shane before X-Pac launches into the Broncobuster; "Yeee haaaaw, ride him cowboy". Shane McMahon is so unbearably awful that he's pushing the envelope to "so bad he's good". Dennis Knight gets clocked with the guitar while X-Pac hits the X-Factor. While nobody is looking Mark Canterbury runs in to lay X-Pac out and Jarrett scores the pin. Another good match! The lumberjacks barely added to the quality, but were at least suitably incorporated into the finish and the setup of it.
Final Rating: **¼

Promo Time: Steve Austin
He's out here to address the title situation. First off the Undertaker, who didn't lie about his one-on-one title match at *SummerSlam* and didn't use his brother's help when he could have done. He bemoans the assaults upon his person and the title so he'll kick everybody's ass. Next up is Ken Shamrock; "Piss on the UFC". "Bring your little blue trunks out here and I'll kick your ass right now". Shamrock responds, but Vince McMahon interjects because he doesn't want to give the match away on *Heat*, and TV time cuts the whole thing off anyway.

THE HEAT RECAP

Most Entertaining: Steve Austin. Damn it, he's even invading the jobber shows and outshining everybody. And it was a decent show!

Least Entertaining: Marc Mero. I'm stunned he got paid to walk into the ring, take one move and then lie around doing nothing.

Quote of the Night: "Don't piss me off? Punk, you're already there" – Jeff Jarrett has been PO'd by X-Pac.

Match of the Night: Ken Shamrock vs. Vader.

Summary: I guess this is what a "good" *Heat* show is like. Two decent matches, a hot angle with Austin - what more can you ask for? They could have done better by just cutting all the crap. The sheer overbooking of Kane vs. D'Lo would have been better off not making it to TV. Same with Val vs. Mero. The show needs streamlining. It's not like these people are getting no exposure anyway. *Heat* can't be mini-*Raw*, it needs its own identity. Other than that criticism, it was pretty good.
Verdict: 35

09.20.98 by Arnold Furious
Venue: Sacramento, CA
Taped: 09.20.98
TV Rating: 3.3

We're in Sacramento, California. A quick aside before we begin regarding the dark match. This was the show that featured on *Beyond the Mat* where indy journeymen Mike Modest and Tony Jones got a WWF tryout. If you've not seen the documentary the director, Barry Blaustein, hangs around backstage while the match is going on and several wrestlers are watching on the monitors. For historical purposes, it'd be great to have that dark match on the broadcast, but seeing as it was just a tryout it's not to be. They'd been repping Roland Alexander's APW. Modest would go on to more success, working for NOAH and WCW before settling into a trainer role himself. Tony Jones got himself a gig working for BattleARTS before working for sleazy garbage fed XPW. He's been back to the WWF but only as a jobber. Jones retired in 2008. On to *Heat* then and hosts for the show are Shane McMahon and Jim Cornette, who is filling in for JR. Unfortunately, that means Shane is handling play-by-play duties.

Mankind vs. Dustin Runnels
Mankind has The Rock and Ken Shamrock in his corner as they've formed a loose alliance to oppose McMahon/Brothers of Destruction. Dustin is going through one of the most dull phases of his entire career, as "plain old Dustin", which isn't someone the fans want to watch. Mick has trouble making the match mean anything, but it's only a few minutes long so luckily no one cares. Double arm DDT sets up the Mandible Claw for the win. Not sure what was with all the nonexistent booking. Why were Rock and Shamrock out there? With Dustin defeated, Val Venis strolls out to torment him further with double entendres regarding his wife's sluttiness. More clips leave Dustin emotionally distraught in the ring. The crowd laugh at him. I despise this feud. Everyone's a damn heel! Who books this crap?
Final Rating: ½*

Backstage: Michael Cole quizzes The Undertaker and Kane about their "business deal" with Vince McMahon. Taker calls it "just business," before threatening Steve Austin and then Cole when he brings up the Babyface Mafia from the first match. Taker threatens them too. Finally Taker turns his attention to DOA, calling them "dead on arrival". Say, more threats? How original. Mankind jumps Kane to break up the interview and he's followed by Rock and Shamrock. This would lead to Vince McMahon switching the booking around to make sure they didn't screw up his masterplan at *Breakdown*, pitting these three against each other. No more Babyface Mafia. Everything settles down and Vince chides Mankind for interrupting his plans. "Well, I feel selfish now, but I *was* hit with a sledgehammer," says Mankind. Vince orders Mankind to leave, taking Shamrock and Rock with him. The Vince-Mankind stuff was gold. Check out the *Heat Recap* for some quotes.

Jacqueline vs. Luna
"Oh Sable, schwing" – Shane. "Insane Clown Posse's rockin' the house". Shane grates at my nerves but he does encourage Jim Cornette to dance, which is cute, before yelling "GO JACQUI, GO JACQUI, GO JACQUI". "She is one tough kitty-kat". Good grief. The match is okay because Jacqui and Luna are actual wrestlers. Unfortunately, the focus is Luna picking up a leg injury and Jacqui working it over. Luna quits to a figure four as Cornette points out that she has historical knee problems. There was nothing technically wrong with this, which makes it better than a lot of WWF ladies matches, but it was short and not particularly fun. Sable calls Jacqueline out so Jacqui challenges her to a wrestling match.
Final Rating: *

Billy Gunn, Triple H & X-Pac vs. Owen Hart, Jeff Jarrett & D'Lo Brown
On paper this looks grand. Billy Gunn is easily the worst worker out there, but it being during DX's peak means he's motivated too. Jim Cornette tries to bury Hunter by saying he'll be in the wrestling business long after Triple H is gone. Guess he didn't account for Hunter marrying into the McMahon dynasty. This was when Road Dogg had an injured throat, so Billy Gunn tries to do the whole introduction instead and botches it. Ah, that makes the cue-cards he uses on the following *Raw* make more sense. Context! D'Lo starts out by bumping like a maniac for Billy Gunn, making him look like a genuine star. Shane finds a new level of annoying by spelling out X-P-A-C instead of saying X-Pac. The two teams make frequent tags as the production team make a few horrible flubs, leading to Jim accusing Kerwin Silfies of drinking. Long-time viewers will remember Kerwin as being mentioned on TV beforehand. He was the man who called in to give Vince an update during the Pillman/Austin/gun debacle. "Who's directing this thing? Hawk?" mocks Shane. He has certain hyena-like qualities. Hunter "injures" his knee and gets picked off for heat, though in reality he already had a knee injury and this match confirmed he needed to take time off. In fact, this is his last outing for more than two months. X-Pac connects with the "bronc-rider" (Cornette) but it all breaks down and Mark Canterbury lays X-Pac out for D'Lo to finish with the Lo Down. Heated match with some logical stuff going on. It would have benefitted from a prolonged opening shine as all the heels are good bumpers, but DX didn't really work like that, because they were all good bumpers too. It almost needed one group to take over and start popping off power moves, like Gunn did with Brown right at the start.
Final Rating: **½

Video Control takes us into the truck where it's revealed that Al Snow was responsible for all the technical glitches in the last match.

Edge vs. TAKA Michinoku
Again? I'm not complaining because it's a good matchup, but TAKA is surely doing too many jobs. Shane spends the introductions moaning that he's "trying to listen to the music". Even when he *is* shutting the fuck up he can't do it right. These guys do the usual lightning quick counters, but Edge catches TAKA with the Downward Spiral after a matter of seconds for the win. Post match, Kaientai run in but Gangrel makes the save. "You will come home," he says as Edge looks at the vampire like he's a hobo offering him out to dinner.
Final Rating: SQUASH

Backstage: Al Snow is carted away in handcuffs. We cut to another *Pacific Blue* shill because Sable is guest starring in a "girls in prison" exploitation episode called 'Heat in the Hole', which is appropriate, seeing as this is *Heat*. Al is brought out to the ring so Sgt. Slaughter can verbally abuse him. "We don't want you within a hundred miles of the WWF", he says before challenging him to a Boot Camp Match on *Raw*. Al is reinstated if he wins. Slaughter beats Al down while he's still handcuffed, and WWF Head of Security Jim Dotson makes the save! Dotson was an onscreen regular during Attitude and it always felt like he was being built up to be a wrestler, but he really *was* a security guy! He never had a match.

The Undertaker & Kane vs. DOA
They must have known this was going to be boring, because Vince McMahon joins commentary to liven things up. Luckily it's kept short, but somehow Shane still manages to be unbearable. They run a horrible spot where Skull

has to break up a pinfall but just stands there in the ring, waiting for the two count before he interjects himself. Why not just break the damn thing before the pin? Kane completely no sells an ugly piledriver and finishes with the Tombstone. Lots of clubberin', but thankfully a lot of power offence down the stretch.
Final Rating: ¼*

THE HEAT RECAP:

Most Entertaining: Mick Foley. His match may have been dull and by-the-numbers but it was over quickly and his backstage antics made the show.

Least Entertaining: Shane McMahon.

Quote of the Night: "I want you to leave. It's for your protection and I want you to take Rock and Ken Shamrock with you"

"Can you give us a ride?"

"What?"

"I don't have…I don't drive"

"….yes". – Vince McMahon an Mankind have a heart-to-heart.

Match of the Night: DX vs. Owen, Jarrett & D'Lo.

Summary: This actually felt like a good show. It had a brisk pace to it, lots of star power and the fans seemed to be into everything. It benefitted from a slightly longer midcard bout with six good wrestlers involved. It's a wee bit disappointing that Edge-TAKA was cut off below the knees and the main event was sloppy, but the storylines were working here. For once, Heat wasn't just a dumping ground; it took storylines from Raw and fleshed them out. Like Al Snow's determination to make it in the WWF, Val Venis' tormenting of Dustin Runnels, and the Babyface Mafia. It helps to connect the dots between big Raw shows, and makes the product feel bigger somehow. More important.
Verdict: 38

09.27.98 by Arnold Furious
Venue: Hamilton, OT
Taped: 09.27.98
TV Rating: 3.3

We're in Hamilton, Ontario. This is the first Heat show I have covered that leads immediately into a PPV, thus the pyro is enormous and the crowd are rabid. Like last week, the hosts are Shane McMahon and Jim Cornette. This airs prior to Breakdown, the culmination of Vince's "masterplan" to rob Steve Austin of the WWF Title. The WWF was in a bit of a creative funk around late summer/early autumn, with Austin stuck against Taker and Kane. However, Breakdown was the show where The Rock, Mick Foley and Ken Shamrock were given their chance to shine, and succeeded in doing so in an excellent three-way dance. The Rock was the guy that shone and ended up with the WWF Title a few months later. Sadly, the road to creative recovery features a lot of tiring Austin-Taker-Kane business in the interim.

Promo Time: Vince McMahon
We kick things off with the chairman of the board. Vince takes the unusual route of apologising to Shamrock, Rock and Mankind (Rock easily getting the biggest pop of the three) for their #1 contender's match getting derailed by Taker and Kane. It's actually his second apology this month, following one to Taker and Kane. By way of apology, Vince books Rock vs. Shamrock vs. Mankind on the PPV in a cage match. McMahon makes a few threats to Austin, including an instant DQ and loss of his title if anyone interferes, before

"guaranteeing" Austin will not leave the ring tonight as WWF Champion.

Sign O' the Times: "Vince, please fire Shane". Amen, brother.

Golga vs. Headbanger Mosh

Despite this being a total scrub match the fans are hot for this. I put it down to ICP's goofy dance-a-long entrance. Sadly the camera doesn't pick up Shane and Cornette dancing along this week. This is Golga's revenge match for the Headbangers "killing" his only friend on *Raw*; a plush Eric Cartman doll. Hey, it's a storyline! The match is decidedly brisk and as soon as Golga gets on top he squashes Mosh with the Vertical Splash. Both 'Bangers get powerbombed post match as the Oddities stand tall. Watching them dance (Luna and Kurrgan especially) is a joyous thing.
Final Rating: ½*

Backstage: Michael Cole tries to report on Triple H being jumped, only for DX to kick him out of the locker room.

Promo Time: Mark Henry

Believe if it or not the original scheduled match on *Breakdown* was Hunter vs. Henry for the IC title. That won't be happening, thanks to Hunter's injury. They must have known Hunter was too injured to compete but booked it anyway. *Card subject to change* and all that. "I came here tonight to impress all of my fans," says Henry pointing out into the audience. "Keep pointing Mark, you'll find one eventually," razzes Cornette. He tells us Hunter is a coward so he's going home, Vince McMahon heads out to calm him down. Vince wants Henry to put the cage to the test on *Heat* to make sure it's up to scratch for the triple threat match. Henry flubs his lines in response as Vince books Mark Henry vs. Steve Austin in a Steel Cage Match as *Heat*'s main event. Mark was okay at reciting pre-scripted lines, but as soon as Vince took it off the script he was completely lost. "I will crush his butt into that rage," was one of the most hilarious flubs.

The Hardy Boyz vs. Men's Teioh & Sho Funaki

The Hardys don't get an entrance, showing where they were in the scheme of things at this stage. However, this era is their big chance to shine, and they happened to arrive at the right time with the right style and right look. They took off in 1999 and became mainstays of the North American scene for over a decade afterwards. This match is so cool it made it onto the WWF's *Wrestling's Highest Fliers* DVD release. Cornette puts over both Hardys' determination and background. They set a blistering pace with Kaientai really taking it to Jeff and the younger Hardy showcasing his bumps. The Hardys bring some cool double teaming including a stereo monkey flip before Jeff tries for a senton *to the floor... which misses!* Talk about putting your body on the line to get yourself noticed! Amazingly he's back up in no time for the Leg Jam/Superfly Splash double team finish. The match could politely be called spotty, but definitely showcased the Hardys as a force to be reckoned with. Humble beginnings here.
Final Rating: **½

Billy Gunn vs. 8-Ball vs. Skull

Gunn volunteered as Steve Austin's partner when no one else would, so Vince has booked him into a similar kind of match that Austin is in tonight as punishment. So while it's booked as a triple threat match, it's actually a handicap match. Billy starts fast but soon finds himself overwhelmed, which shows the crowd exactly how disappointing tonight's PPV main event will be. Vince also threw in another similar stipulation banning X-Pac and

Road Dogg from interfering. As Jim Cornette tries to explain the importance of the stipulations, Shane McMahon cuts him off again and again and again and again. Mainly to call punches and kicks, which is the entire match. He is insufferable and virtually impossible to work with. Gunn eventually lies down after about five minutes of boring offence. DX run in to stop the two-on-one, but Southern Justice follow and DX get laid out. The only good thing about this was Cornette trying in vain to make the storylines make sense. He was doing a hell of a job of it too. Everything else was horrible, especially Shane who was awful here. He has no apparent understanding of the business or the importance of what Cornette was conveying.

Final Rating: DUD

Backstage: Chyna jumps Mark Henry and beats him down with a steel bar, thus cancelling tonight's scheduled main event. Bait and switch, bait and switcheroo. You can't even deliver the match you booked less than an hour ago? In the ring the cage is locked by a technician, who strongly resembles Arn Anderson, but reveals himself to be a disguised Steve Austin. He beats McMahon down until Taker and Kane climb into the cage and run him off. After a final shill for the PPV, Vince grabs the microphone once more to again guarantee that Austin won't leave the arena with the WWF Title tonight.

THE HEAT RECAP:

Most Entertaining: Despite a couple of decent Vince promos, I'm going with the Hardy Boyz. They certainly took their opportunity.

Least Entertaining: Shane McMahon. With each week and each show, he puts forward a case for being the worst commentator of all time. I'm struggling to think of guys who are worse. Maybe Mark Madden. There was a UWF team featuring Herb Abrams and Lou Albano, which was an embarrassment, but at least it was amusing. Shane is amongst those guys. He's the shits.

Quote of the Night: "My only regret is that tonight's PPV extravaganza has to take place here in Canada" – Vince McMahon, always welcome north of the border.

Match of the Night: The Hardy Boyz vs. Kaientai

Summary: The WWF was on shill duty here, and while that made *Heat* feel more relevant than usual, it also reduced the wrestling time considerably. The main reason for watching was the hype, so the show had a lot of talking, especially from Vince McMahon. Though, it doesn't make sense to me for them to set up a main event with an in-ring promo and then not do it at all. It's just a waste of time. The in-ring was mixed as well, with two really bad matches, the Billy Gunn one being an abomination, but on the flip side a very solid showing from the Hardy Boyz. I'd rather there was more wrestling on the show, as ever, but I understand the need for building the PPV. They tried to make *Breakdown* un-missable with the pre-show antics, but unfortunately it was not a PPV I had much interest in.

Verdict: 31

10.04.98 by Lee Maughan
Venue: East Lansing, MI
Taped: 09.29.98
TV Rating: 3.8

- Hosted by Shane McMahon and Jim Cornette.

X-Pac vs. Owen Hart
These two have had some quality outings over the years, but there are so

many storyline strands surrounding this one it's hard to believe the match won't get smothered by at least one of them. Firstly, there appears to be dissension in the DX ranks after Road Dogg intentionally got the New Age Outlaws disqualified in a match against Southern Justice on *Raw* earlier in the week. That led to a heated argument during which Gunn inadvertently belted X-Pac in his injured eye before walking out in frustration. Secondly, D'Lo Brown has joined the commentary team, having won a six-man elimination match over the motley crew of Edge, 'Marvellous' Marc Mero, Jeff Jarrett, Droz and Gangrel on that same edition of *Raw*, earning himself a crack at X-Pac's gold on tomorrow's episode; Thirdly, and perhaps most importantly of all, Owen is down in the dumps having sent Dan Severn out of *Raw* on a stretcher in a re-enactment of his all-too-real sitout piledriver that temporarily paralyzed Steve Austin at *SummerSlam* '97. Thankfully the situation with Severn is just a bad taste angle, the outcome of which would result in one of the most unfortunate tragedies in wrestling history. For now it's the third of those strands that has the most bearing on the quality of the bout, as Owen just has no heart left in him and refuses to fight back. X-Pac's dropkick, bodyslam and leg drop are all nice and crisp, but just when you're hoping a forgotten classic will break out, X-Pac misses a charge in the corner, and Owen walks off. X-Pac goes out after him and fires him back inside, but misses another charge and Owen leaves again to really hammer the point home. This time X-Pac just drags him back to the ring and pins him with a roll-up as D'Lo prophetically promises to win Pac's belt. A real disappointment for anyone hoping for an action-packed bout, as this existed simply to further Owen's depression angle.
Final Rating: *¼

- This past week on *Raw*, Steve Austin got himself carted off to jail after driving a zamboni into the arena and attacking Mr. McMahon. In response, McMahon announced an Undertaker vs. Kane match for *Judgment Day* for the vacant WWF Title with Austin as the special guest referee. Unfortunately for Vince, he made the mistake of flipping 'Taker and Kane the bird after they warned him not to cross them, so they broke his leg and sent him to the hospital, where he presumably shared a ward with Dan Severn. Hopefully he won't leave any bedpans laying around.

Sho Funaki vs. Matt Hardy

This comes about after the Hardy Boyz beat Kaientai last week in what was actually considered an upset. Matt scores early with a plancha but misses an elbow off the top, only to come back with a crucifix bomb and a top rope lionsault, showing some really amazing athleticism. Funaki returns fire with a fisherman suplex and lands a flying headbutt off the top to win it at a ludicrously short 2:10.
Final Rating: **

The Oddities vs. The Headbangers

This is a grudge match after Kurrgan and Golga beat the Headbangers on *Raw* when the Insane Clown Posse tripped Mosh from the outside, causing Kurrgan to get the pin. Whatever you think of ICP, however you feel about their lyrical content ("Fuckin' magnets, how do they work?"), however you feel about their dismissive opinion of science ("Fuckin' magnets, how do they work?"), and however you feel about their abrasive attitudes in general ("Fuckin' magnets, how do they work?"), at least they're a step up from Oscar when it comes to rapping a tag team out to the ring.

The match is about the most basic tag

bout you'll ever see, with the babyfaces each taking a turn to shine against one of their opponents, Golga missing a charge in the corner to put the Headbangers on offence, a brief double team behind the referee's back, ICP pushing Thrasher off the top as Kurrgan has the referee distracted to turn back the tide, and Golga pinning Mosh with the sit-down splash. All the while, Shane and Cornette ignore the action to put over *Pacific Blue*, *Silk Stalkings* and *La Femme Nikita* instead. Phew!
Final Rating: *

- Steven Regal moves mountains, and he's a Real Man's Man.

DOA vs. Mankind & Ken Shamrock

Well aware that nobody gets much time on *Heat*, DOA jump Shamrock before the bell and immediately go into the, well, heat. Shamrock and Mankind are being forced to team up here, having been opponents in a triple threat cage match with The Rock at *Breakdown* last Sunday, and that comes into play when Shamrock makes a grumpy tag that puts Mankind on the receiving end of DOA's tedious clubberin'. Mankind stays alive with a clothesline and comes back from a second round of heat with a double arm DDT. Mankind looks to drop an elbow from that but Paul Ellering trips him from outside, so Mankind puts him in the Mandible Claw. That gives Shamrock the opening to run around the ring and smash his partner over the head with a steel chair, giving DOA what might legitimately be one of the biggest wins of their career, name value -wise.
Final Rating: *

- Steve Austin heads out to the production truck with an axe and cuts off a satellite feed to Mr. McMahon's hospital bed, then comes out to join the commentary team.

The Rock vs. Jeff Jarrett

These two take a cue from DOA and don't bother waiting for the bell, with Rock landing a Samoan drop but missing a charge into the corner. It is the fourth time someone has run that transition in five matches tonight. Jarrett scores with a beautiful flying clothesline, misses a dropkick, but quickly comes back with a running neckbreaker. Sadly the announcers again ignore the action, this time because Mr. McMahon has called in to bicker with Austin, and they miss outside interference from Dennis Knight. Rock rolls through a high cross to stay alive and counters a suplex with one of his own, leading to a floatover DDT and the People's Elbow to an enormous reaction. That looks to do it, but Knight pulls the referee out from the floor in yet another overdone wrestling trope (the fourth such instance tonight if you include the Oddities-Headbangers flashback from *Raw*, which is three times too many on a sixty-minute show), so Austin decides to show his authoritative side ahead of *Judgment Day* and drops the heels with two Stone Cold Stunners before going face-to-face with Rock to a thunderous response. If that was the WWF testing the waters on the potential of an Austin-Rock match headlining *WrestleMania XV*, then this crowd certainly gave them the reaction they were looking for. And then some.
Final Rating: ***

THE HEAT RECAP:

Most Entertaining: Funaki and Matt Hardy. I'll admit I might be cheating here because I thought Rock-Jarrett was easily the match of the night. But Funaki and Hardy had about as good a two-minute match as you're ever likely to see, so I figured they deserved singling out for some special praise.

Least Entertaining: DOA, who unlike Jeff Jarrett, did absolutely nothing remotely exciting or interesting while they were on offence.

Quote of the Night: "I'm the best thing that's happened to Europe since Napoleon!" - D'Lo Brown.

Match of the Night: The Rock vs. Jeff Jarrett. A really energetic performance from both guys, with an ending that left one salivating at the prospect of another run of Rock vs. Austin matches.

Summary: One could very rightly moan about the scant amount of time most of the matches got tonight, and about the tepid performance of DOA, but this was a pretty fun show overall. The X-Pac vs. Owen Hart non-match was a disappointment, sure, but it felt like everything on the show mattered, at least in some small way, and had a reason for existing. A red-hot crowd hurt didn't either. As far as throwaway weekend B-show wrestling TV goes, this one is pretty recommended.
Verdict: 38

10.11.98 by Lee Maughan
Venue: East Lansing, MI
Taped: 09.29.98
TV Rating: 3.6

- Hosted by Shane McMahon and Jim Cornette.

WWF Women's Championship
Jacqueline (c) vs. Starla Saxton
Jacqueline has a weave of Sable's blonde hair tied into her ponytail, and this is her first title defence according to Shane. That isn't exactly true, as she'd defended it at the previous evening's taping for the international version of *Shotgun Saturday Night* against... Starla Saxton! What Saxton has done to earn a title shot here is anybody's guess, as Cornette erroneously calls this her first WWF match. Obviously, that appearance doesn't "count" in the WWF's televisual world, but it still doesn't explain why she got this title match, or the other one for that matter. She looks seriously dated too, sporting a garishly bright ladies-style wetsuit straight out of early nineties LLPW. Saxton actually gets a little bit of offence in, scoring a roll-up off a collision between Jacqueline and 'Marvellous' Marc Mero on the apron, before landing a really nice bridging double underhook suplex for two. It's all for naught however as Jackie steals the Rock's floatover DDT for the pin. Not to worry though, as Saxton would be back in a couple of years, albeit under a different name - Molly Holly. As for poor Jacqueline, Sable dashes out to the ring and big boots her square in the face.
Final Rating: **

Kaientai vs.
Too Much & The Hardy Boyz
The Hardys have been going back and forth with Kaientai over recent weeks, but the presence of Too Much for this atomicos outing is explained as being at the whim of Mr. McMahon. Yeah, right, like he cares about filler matches on *Heat*! Scott Taylor starts out with a pumphandle suplex on Taka Michinoku, then moonwalks his way over to the corner to tag in Brian Christopher, allowing Christopher to resume his hostilities with Taka via a side Russian face plant. Jeff Hardy comes in with a sweet springboard moonsault press on Teioh, and the Hardys follow that with Poetry in Motion. Christopher comes back in with a sitout powerbomb on Funaki and Too Much look to finish it with that old Midnight Express classic the Veg-O-Matic (an assisted guillotine leg drop combo) on Teioh, as called by Cornette. That brings all eight guys in, but Funaki comes off the top with a diving headbutt amidst the confusion, and puts Teioh on top of Taylor for the pin. At least, that was the plan; Funaki actually missed his dive and killed the

finish completely, though I'd say the biggest flaw was giving eight guys three minutes to play with. Too Much attack the Hardys afterwards, so that looks to be the new *Heat*-exclusive program.
Final Rating: *¼

- This past week on *Raw*, Mankind showed up at Mr. McMahon's hospital bedside with Yurple the Clown and her wacky balloon animal tricks. More significantly, he also unleashed Mr. Socko upon the world.

Edge vs. Vader
Talk about two guys on opposite sides of a career trajectory. Edge had made his on-screen in-ring debut for the WWF just a few months prior to this and was en route (eventually) to the very top of the WWE mountain, while this is actually Vader's last televised match in the WWF, at least until his brief return in 2005 to put over Batista.

The psychology comes across as somewhat backwards for whatever reason, as Vader is clearly working as a bully heel and Edge is obviously a babyface, but it's Vader who gets the shine, stiffing the daylights out of Edge with body shots, a powerbomb and a clothesline, while Edge gets the heat by hurling Vader into the steel steps. I suppose if you were to truncate things, you could say that Edge never got a shine, they went right into the heat, and then Edge began mounting his comeback, which is probably a better way of looking at things when you consider his big moves consist of a leaping spinning heel kick and a flying clothesline, two decidedly blue eye manoeuvres. Vader then catches him coming off the top with a monstrous powerslam but misses a vertical splash, and Edge hits the Downward Spiral (a reverse STO) for the pin in what Cornette dubs an "upset". Vader stuck around for a little while after this, tapping out to Ken Shamrock in a triple threat match with Mankind at the October 25th Madison Square Garden house show, before heading off to rebuild his reputation in Japan.
Final Rating: **

Al Snow vs. Ken Shamrock
Snow gets in a token clothesline early on, but Shamrock quickly blasts him with a belly-to-belly suplex and slaps on the ankle lock. Snow, laughing, grabs the bottom rope with his teeth, but Shamrock refuses to break so it's a DQ already. Scorpio comes out to try and make the save for Snow, but he too eats a belly-to-belly. Shamrock puts the ankle lock back on Snow, drawing out Mankind with a steel chair, which sends Shamrock fleeing. Not really a match as such, just an excuse for an angle.
Final Rating: ½*

- "Concentrate. You won't find this man pouring juice from a cardboard container, oh no, he squeezes his own hand-selected Florida oranges and savours his extraction, pulp and all! He's Steven Regal, a Real Man's Man!"

Jeff Jarrett vs. Road Dogg
This is a rematch from the September 14th *Raw* where Jarrett pinned Road Dogg after bashing him up good with pieces of a broken guitar, though Cornette adds more spice to the proceedings by referencing the "Milli Vanilli" fake singing period of 'The Real Double J'. At least we aren't subjected to another blast of *'With My Baby Tonight'*. On a roll, Cornette brings up Jerry Jarrett and 'Bullet' Bob Armstrong as Shane dutifully ignores him, even as Corny stops to put him over as a fourth generation McMahon. Dogg works in his Doggy elbow but Jarrett takes over with a high cross. He crotches himself on the middle rope however, and Dogg smashes Jarrett's own guitar over his head for the quick DQ in pro wrestling's

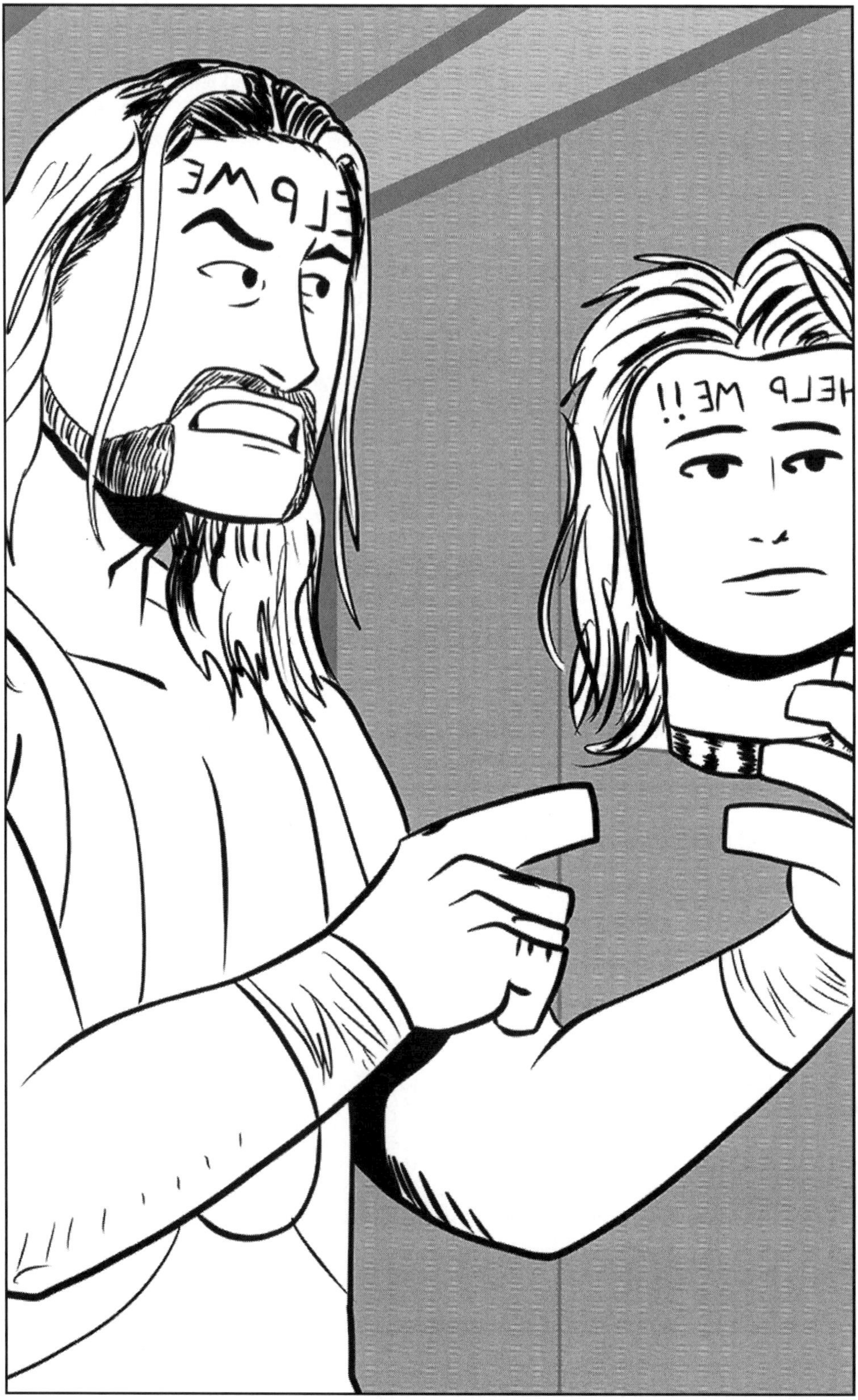
HELP ME!!

ultimate act of serendipitous happenstantial revenge. Or something.
Final Rating: ½*

- Back again to *Raw* for the classic skit in which Dr. Austin attacked Mr. McMahon in his hospital bed, pounded his broken leg, zapped him with defibrillator paddles (surely grounds for attempted murder?), shoved a surgical tube up his anus (surely grounds for sexual assault?) and clobbered him over the head with a bedpan with a hilariously satisfying "KLANG!"

Steve Austin vs. D'Lo Brown
D'Lo regained the European title from X-Pac on *Raw* thanks to a trip from Mark Henry on the outside (what else?), but this is non-title, for obvious reasons. The match is another two-minute special as Austin runs through his key spots (punches, two suplexes, Thesz press, second rope elbow) and gives D'Lo absolutely nothing before finishing it with a Stone Cold Stunner. Now, I'm not saying you shouldn't book Austin in that manner, but surely you can find someone other than your new European Champion to play the whipping boy? Mark Henry eats a Stunner after the match too, and that's it for the show, stay tuned to the USA Network to see Sable get banged... up in a women's prison on *Pacific Blue*!
Final Rating: *

THE HEAT RECAP:

Most Entertaining: I'd be tempted to give it to the Mr. McMahon hospital skits from *Raw*, but that feels like a cheat, so we'll say Edge and Vader for at least having a halfway competitive match.

Least Entertaining: Nobody, really. The upside to nobody getting enough time to cobble together a decent match is that nobody got enough time to wear out their welcome either.

Quote of the Night: "Some what?" - Shane McMahon displays all the same aptitude for the finer points of pro wrestling as his old man ever did, in response to Jim Cornette lavishing praise upon Jacqueline and Starla Saxton for "some good chain wrestling".

Match of the Night: Edge vs. Vader. The only thing even resembling a worthwhile match on the entire show this week, and a good, solid win for Edge to boot.

Summary: We're still in the era of getting actual big-name stars on *Heat* which I appreciate, but six matches for an hour-long show already filled with *Raw* flashback videos is just too much, especially when the era of the squash match is all but over. Nothing had time to develop, and the only matches that didn't feel overcrowded were the Women's Title match and the Edge vs. Vader bout, both fairly competitive singles matches noticeably devoid of run-ins, angles and interference. Everything else was just too short, and the idea of giving eight of your more energetic workers just three minutes is utterly infuriating.
Verdict: 26

10.18.98 by Lee Maughan
Venue: Chicago, IL
Taped: 10.18.98
TV Rating: 4.7

- Hosted by Shane McMahon and Jim Cornette, and there's a little different feel to the show tonight as this is the monthly pay-per-view pre-show episode, tonight leading in to *Judgment Day*.

Steve Blackman vs. Bradshaw
On the orders of Mr. McMahon, Blackman returned from injury on *Raw* against the advice of his doctor, where

he tapped out to Ken Shamrock. Blackman doesn't bother selling his knee however, which makes me wonder why they bothered showing that clip. Bradshaw doesn't even get an entrance here and is already in the ring when Blackman gets introduced, which becomes a running theme for the night. Cornette at least tries to put him over as having started to add more moves to his repertoire, displaying an incredible knack for comic timing as the crowd begin chanting "Bradshaw sucks!" in earnest. One of the turds in the audience even starts wailing "Boring! Boring!" at the top of his lungs, despite both guys putting forth a decent effort. Thankfully, nobody else joins in, hopefully leaving a strong feeling of shame in the pit of his stomach. It'd be one thing if they were sitting around in chinlocks, but between them they break out a fallaway slam, a bodyslam, a gut wrench suplex and flying shoulderblock. Hardly boring fare for a quickie *Heat* match. Blackman blasts Bradshaw in the face with a scissors kick to take the honours, only to get attacked from behind by the mysterious Blue Blazer.
Final Rating: *½

The Oddities vs. Los Boricuas

Naturally, it's the Boricuas who don't get an entrance here. This basically exists to fill time and to promote the "battle of the boom box" between the New Age Outlaws and the Headbangers on the pay-per-view later on, as the Headbangers have had an ongoing issue with the Oddities lately. Jose Estrada and Miguel Perez double team Golga to start, who comes back with a double clothesline and brings in Kurrgan. Kurrgan was one of those guys who always came in for a lot of flack over his in-ring abilities, but in truth, he's much better than a lot of other wrestling giants. He's no Andre the Giant or Big Show certainly, but he's much, much better than the likes of El Gigante/Giant Gonzalez, the Great Khali and, erm, Giant Silva. Which is a shame, since he tags in next. Thankfully they limit him to a single powerbomb before Golga comes back in to completely expose himself by doing the Earthquake running vertical splash for the pin. That brings out the Headbangers to beat the life out of the Insane Clown Posse to the delight of music fans everywhere, which in turn is the perfect excuse to bring out the Outlaws for a brawl in the aisle.
Final Rating: *½

The Godfather vs. Faarooq

What an indignation this is, as Faarooq, former leader of the Nation of Domination, is "his opponent, in the corner to my left" while the Godfather, former follower of the Nation of Domination, is the guy who gets an actual introduction. He's still working to get the pimp gimmick over so he's offers Faarooq the choice of one of his two ho's, but Faarooq attacks him instead. Bizarrely, Shane and Cornette take a moment to put over tonight's episodes of *Pacific Blue*, *Silk Stalkings* and *La Femme Nikita* on USA Network, just in case you wanted an alternative to watching *Judgment Day* I guess. Contractual obligations and all that. D'Lo Brown and Mark Henry come out to observe, having kicked the Rock out of the Nation on *Raw*, just in time to see Faarooq get crotched on the top and kicked in the face for the pin. D'Lo whomps Godfather with the Sky High after the match and Henry gives him a big splash, all as an excuse to have the Rock sprint out to ringside and chase them away.
Final Rating: *¼

- During the break, the Jackyl made his return to the WWF to confer with Faarooq. Speaking from experience, Cornette notes: "You always make your pick when the guy's down in the dumps.

You never go to him when he's on top, you go to him when he's vulnerable and has a psychological need."

Scorpio vs. Jeff Jarrett

Poor old Scorpio isn't just "in the ring, his opponent...", as Jarrett comes out, he also has to stand there as special guest commentator Val Venis gets an entrance too! They trade waistlocks to start and Scorpio shows his flashy, funky style with a nice backflip and a dropkick, but they annoyingly cut away to ringside where Goldust's usher from his aborted 1996 feud with Razor Ramon shows up with a mystery box for Venis. Hilariously, he wipes his presumably now effluence-covered glove across his jacket while shooting Venis a look of pure disgust after touching the jizz-stained superstar. Scorpio misses a flying crossbody and Jarrett clotheslines him to the floor, following with a baseball slide, but they cut away again a Venis dips his fingers in the box and has a fiddle around, producing a gold athletic cup. Given that Goldust likes to kick his opponents in the scrotum, and given that Venis has a second career built entirely around his dong, you think he'd be chuffed with that, but instead he just storms off.

Naturally, with that momentum-killing distraction out of the way, Jarrett chooses to get the bout back on track by sitting in a chinlock. You would think that whoever agented this match might have saved the Venis stuff for the chinlock spot and made sure the action portion of the bout was caught on camera, but no. Scorpio goes for a jumping twisting kick to the face, and the referee gets bumped of all things. In this match! That brings out Al Snow, who ludicrously hides Head in the back pocket of the referee, who somehow fails to notice that he's got a mannequin head lodged between his buttocks. For some reason the sight of that distracts Jarrett long enough for Scorpio to pin him with a roll-up from behind. A truly suspension of disbelief-stretching finish to a match that might have been pretty good aside from the best part of it being completely ignored for a comedy bit that wasn't all that funny. Blergh.

Final Rating: *

- Backstage, the Stooges make Steve Austin change in a closet with the referees instead of the wrestlers ahead of his refereeing tonight's Undertaker vs. Kane WWF Title match at *Judgment Day*.

- With Triple H's knee injury and inability to defend his Intercontinental Title, he has been stripped of his gold. As per the orders of Mr. McMahon, he has to hand the belt over to Ken Shamrock, who won an eight man elimination tournament on *Raw*, beating Steve Blackman, Val Venis and X-Pac along the way. Hunter comes out and hands it over like Shawn Michaels after a particularly heavy night on the tiles with the marines, then tells Shamrock to "suck it!"

- Back from the break, Shamrock catches up to Triple H in the parking lot and slams a car door on his injured knee.

- Mr. McMahon rolls out to ringside in his wheelchair to eat up the last few minutes before the pay-per-view goes live with a rant against Austin and the fans, telling Austin he'll never get a rematch for the WWF Title.

THE HEAT RECAP:

Most Entertaining: Nobody. Nobody was any better or worse than anyone else on the show, and nobody in particular stood out.

Least Entertaining: Nobody. See

"Most Entertaining".

Quote of the Night: "Who booked this shit?" - Not so much a quote as a presumptive fan with an amusing sign.

Match of the Night: Wow. Let's do the unthinkable and give it to Giant Silva and pals, on account of ignorance. The cameras ignored Scorpio-Jarrett, the announcers ignored Godfather-Faarooq, and Steve Blackman ignored his previous knee injury in the match with Bradshaw. Plus, I'm rather tickled at the thought of Los Boricuas actually winning a match of the night award.

Summary: Obviously this show was designed to hype up *Judgment Day*, and to that end it did a decent enough job. But the problem with doing a live lead-in for a pay-per-view is that all your big stars are booked for the main show, leaving your plate with a meal thrown together from the leftover scraps. An entirely skippable show.
Verdict: 26

10.25.98 by Lee Maughan
Venue: Milwaukee, WI
Taped: 10.19.98
TV Rating: 4.0

- Hosted by Michael Cole and Jim Cornette, with Shane McMahon apparently taking the night off.

WWF Light Heavyweight Championship
Christian (c) vs. Brian Christopher
Christian won the title from Taka Michinoku last week at *Judgment Day* in his "first WWF match" (Jay Reso actually made his real WWF debut as Christian Cage in a dark match loss to the future Edge, Adam Copeland, at the November 11th, 1997 RAW taping in Cornwall, Ontario, Canada), and this is his first defence, somewhat ironically against the man who Taka defeated to win the title in the first place. Like Starla Saxton against Jacqueline a couple of weeks ago, also purported to be having her first match in the WWF, they don't actually bother to come with an explanation for how or why Christian got a title shot on his first night in. With Taka out of the picture, it's safe to say the belt is firmly lodged in "WWF style" now, with the only high-flying from Christopher a missed second rope crossbody. Christian's a little more game for it with a super huracánrana off the top, though it's a touch sluggish when compared the ones being broken out on a weekly basis over in WCW's cruiserweight ranks. He adds a pair of rolling suplexes which are topped with a nice sitout gourdbuster but misses a splash of the top. That sends Christopher to the top but he whiffs on the Tennessee Jam, and Christian finishes him with his double underhook face buster, soon to be named the Impaler, later to be named the Unprettier, and eventually to be named the Killswitch. Gangrel adds to the fun by punching Scott Taylor in the face for no particular reason.
Final Rating: **

Jeff Jarrett vs. Golga
Jarrett is quietly becoming the mainstay of *Sunday Night Heat*, this being his fourth consecutive match on the show, and his ninth overall in just thirteen weeks. He's also got his old WCW valet Debra McMichael with him after she debuted on *Raw* this past week. Cornette takes the time to put Jarrett over as a twelve-year veteran despite only being thirty, mentions Golga's relative lack of smarts, and even stops off to bury Michael Cole, much to my personal delight. Golga's size is too much for Jarrett in the early going, and he goes to work with an elbow drop, a leg drop and a bodyslam, but goes over the top to the floor on a charge attempt. Jarrett goes after him with a baseball

slide and a flying clothesline, but makes the mistake of ramming Golga's head into the turnbuckles, which he no-sells in grand Samoan fashion. A big boot and a powerslam follow, but he gets distracted before he can land the running vertical splash when Debra throws his Cartman plush at him, thus paying off Cornette's earlier words. Jarrett drops him with his reverse Russian leg sweep for the pin.
Final Rating: **

The Headbangers vs. DOA

The Headbangers are embroiled in a feud with the New Age Outlaws at this point, so they do a half-hearted parody with foam title belts, their own take on the "Oh you didn't know?" ring introduction, and Mosh working in Dogg's Boogie Woogie elbow. Even though both teams are heels, the Headbangers work the match as babyfaces, which seems like an odd route to go down when they're the act being featured in a program against a babyface duo. Worse still, the Headbangers working the babyface role means sitting through another round of the DOA's frequently tedious heat, made up as it is of boots, elbows and punches. Truly thrilling stuff. The Headbangers at least offer mild excitement when Thrasher powerbombs Mosh onto one of the twins, and there's actually a pretty decent finish... sort of. DOA switch off illegally but the referee gets distracted by Paul Ellering on the apron, allowing the Headbangers to backdrop the illegal guy over the top and pin the legal one with a roll-up, unsurprisingly drawing a tepid response from the crowd. That finish might have actually gotten over if they'd done it fifteen years earlier in the NWA where going over the top was a disqualification, but this is the WWF in 1998 so nobody gives a shit.
Final Rating: *

- And now for the thing we all tune in to pro wrestling for - middle aged pop metal a decade-and-a-half past its sell by date! Yes, Vince Neil, Tommy Lee and their whole Mötley Crüe are on hand to rock the house with '*Bitter Pill*', an original cut from their new Greatest Hits LP. The melody is nice enough but the lyrics are completely cringe-worthy, sounding like they were written by an inexperienced fifteen-year old who just got his first Squier Stratocaster and Fender practice amp for Christmas. "The fans are enjoying it!" notes a surprised Cole, as lashings of fake cheers are dubbed over the performance. Still, if it wasn't for this the world would never have been introduced to their "bodyguard", who drags an invading fan off the stage with a full Nelson. His name? Test.

- Last week on *Raw*, Steve Austin pointed a pop gun at Mr. McMahon's head, pulled the trigger revealing a Bang 3:16 sign, and watched Vince piss his pants. Vince calls in and tells the fans, Cole and Cornette all to go to hell. At least they'll get to settle their issues this Thursday in a singles bout on MTV's *Celebrity Deathmatch*.

- Scorpio comes out for a match but the Blue Blazer chokes him out with a Dragon sleeper, a move Dan Severn rather conspicuously taught to Owen Hart.

- Cornette reveals the first names for the upcoming WWF Title tournament at *Survivor Series: Deadly Game* - The Rock, The Undertaker, and The Big Bossman.

Ken Shamrock & D'Lo Brown vs. Mankind & X-Pac

X-Pac has regained the European title from D'Lo Brown, having beaten him at last week's *Judgment Day* pay-per-view, but he's lost Chyna due to a sexual harassment suit filed against her by Mary Henry. Surely he should have done that after she knowingly set him up with Sammi the transvestite to humiliate him? These four guys all mesh really well together despite the mix of styles, with two very lively babyfaces showing a lot of fire, and two heels prepared to break out a varied array of moves (the highlights being leaping leg lariats from Shamrock and D'Lo's Sky High) to keep the fans interested. DOA take note.

They also get a decent amount of time to develop things, at least per the usual *Sunday Night Heat* standards (i.e. more than five minutes), and there's a very audible "Oooh!" from the crowd when Mankind gets the hot tag and runs wild on his opponents but gets carried away and punches out X-Pac too. That gives Shamrock an opening to slap the ankle lock on Mankind, but X-Pac saves him before wiping out D'Lo with a slingshot plancha on the floor. Back in the ring, Mankind comes back with a double arm DDT and a Socko-assisted Mandible Claw. That leads to a terrific finish in which Shamrock counters with a belly-to-back suplex and gets the pin, but only because Mankind refuses to give up the Claw, causing Shamrock to pass out before the three count has even registered. "I lost the match... but there's your winner!" gloats an apologetic Mankind afterwards, with Shamrock soon reviving, throwing a fit of anger, and audibly yelling "Fuck!" at the crowd. This was great!
Final Rating: ***

THE HEAT RECAP:

Most Entertaining: Mankind edges it thanks to a an amusing pre-match promo and his deranged ramblings after eating the pinfall loss. Ken Shamrock deserves a special mention too for his post-Claw rage around ringside. In fact, all the guys in the main event were very good this week.

Least Entertaining: DOA. If Skull and 8-Ball are in action, there's a strong chance they'll be automatic candidates for the Least Entertaining award.

Quote of the Night: "If you're not down with that, we got two words for ya... You suck!" / "If you're not down with that, we got one word for ya... Socko!" - Thrasher and Mankind put their own personal spins on the Road Dogg's quotable introductory speech.

Match of the Night: Ken Shamrock & D'Lo Brown vs. Mankind & X-Pac. Star power + good workers + time to develop + distinct lack of overbooked silliness + clean finish = good match. It's pro wrestling, it's ain't rocket science.

Summary: Not a bad little waste of an hour this week, with the best *Heat* match since The Rock vs. Jeff Jarrett three weeks ago, and the announcing of a trio of big names for the upcoming *Deadly Game* tournament making it feel like something of genuine importance was happening.
Verdict: 48

11.01.98 by James Dixon

Venue: Austin, TX
Taped: 11.01.98
TV Rating: 3.3

We are live from Texas, and hosts tonight are Michael Cole and Jim Cornette. We have gone from one bad/good pairing straight into another. Why can't they get it right? Ross and Cornette is the answer, how is that not obvious?

The Legion of Doom
vs. The Hardy Boyz

I guess in later years some might consider this a dream match of sorts,

though the Hardys at their peak are in no way comparable to the Road Warriors in their pomp. The Hardys were far more exciting, sure, but the Roadies are legendary. As usual of late, Droz is the partner of choice for Animal, which leads to almost immediate dissention between Droz and Hawk. After bumping around for Animal, the Hardys then take him out and beat him with their legdrop/splash top rope combo. The Hardy Boyz beat the LOD! What a world. Post match, Hawk promises to "kick the stinking puke" out of Droz on tomorrow night's *Raw*. Interesting opener for historical purposes, but too brief and storyline driven to be anything more than a curio.
Final Rating: *¼

Steven Regal vs. Bradshaw
The ludicrous "real man's man" Regal heads to the ring to throw out an open challenge to anyone in the "WWWF" to answer his challenge. He would have been a really good fit for the company in the seventies, actually. Hometown boy Bradshaw answers the challenge and wastes little time laying into him. Regal takes a while to find his groove, and when he does Cornette calls him one of the top three wrestlers to ever come out of Britain, behind Billy Robinson and the Dynamite Kid. Davey Boy Smith was persona non grata at this point having walked out with Bret Hart post-Montreal so that one is directly from Vince. Regal wins with a cradle back suplex out of nowhere, prompting Cole to note that, "Regal, and his music, have won here". Odd comment. Nothing match.
Final Rating: ½*

The Oddities vs. The Brood
The prospect of this is inexplicably appealing. Kurrgan's first move is a Bossman Slam, which I guess sets the tone for what we will be getting here: moves! Lots of them with no substance or logic attached. A minute or so in, Michael Cole loses his mind and starts seeing apparitions clad in red hanging around in the rafters. Corny assumes it is Kane, watching the bout looking for revenge after the Brood beat him up on *Raw*. I assume that Cole is just a gum-flapping goofball. Strangely enough, this is not the first time that Gangrel and Golga have wrestled on WWF television. They had a match on *Raw* back in 1994, only Golga was then known as Earthquake and Gangrel was jobber The Black Phantom. Shenanigans on the outside lead to distraction and Gangrel pins his old foe, writing the wrongs in his record book from 1994. Far too short, as ever.
Final Rating: ¾*

D'Lo Brown vs. Steve Blackman
These two don't waste any time getting right into the big hitting action, obviously mindful that time is of a premium on this show. About a minute in Brown hits his running powerbomb, but then inexplicably doesn't go for the cover because the Headbangers walk down and do... nothing. Instead he does a contrived spot where he climbs to the top for the frogsplash, only to be pushed off by a 'Banger and cradled by Blackman for the win. It felt so obvious and forced that D'Lo only went for the frogsplash to enable the Headbangers to play a part, because otherwise he had the match won. This was the shortest bout yet.
Final Rating: ¾*

Meanwhile, Michael Cole tries to grab an interview with Dan Severn from his home, but the feed isn't working. These are the risks of going live, I'm afraid.

Jeff Jarrett vs. Val Venis
Sadly the match here is mere background noise for the real purpose: furthering some mundane bitchy issue that Debra and Terri Runnels have with each other. Who cares? Neither of them

are wrestlers, so where is the payoff? Some sort of degrading stripper match? I find both utterly vile. Terri's presence serves to be an albatross for Val, who gets beaten following her accidental distraction. Terri immediately apologises, but asks Val to focus on the positives. She says they have created joy together, then reveals she is pregnant. Oh, it's *that* angle. Cole shrieks with glee like an excited little girl as Cornette does his best to put over an angle he despised. Val, being Val, tells Terri it is her problem not his, and he bails. There's your babyface, folks.
Final Rating: ½*

Live via satellite, we have Dan Severn at the second time of asking. "Well, I have been better," he says deadpan when asked about his condition following Owen Hart "crippling" him with a piledriver. Severn, softly spoken and calm, tells Owen he will be at *Raw* tomorrow with some choice words and advises him to be there. For such a tough guy, Severn has one of the least intimidating voices you will ever hear in pro wrestling.

Promo Time: Shane McMahon

McMahon-a-Mania is running wild tonight, as we endure the fallout of Shane McMahon growing a set on *Raw* and confronting his dad. It was one of the most cringe-worthy pieces of nepotistic garbage that I have been forced to sit through on the show. How lucky for us that since he has departed from commentating, he has been given an even bigger role on television. Naturally, Shane's promo goes far longer than any of the matches have tonight, because god knows I want to hear Shane McMahon put himself over for ten minutes far more than I want to see some wrestling. I might care more about this if it didn't ultimately become completely meaningless later in the month when Shane revealed it to all be a ruse, and that he was aligned with his father all along.

The Godfather vs. The Undertaker

Oh here it is, the *SummerSlam '95* rematch that no-one wanted to see. The match is at least semi notable for being Undertaker's first match with Paul Bearer back at his side since *SummerSlam '96*. Yes, lots of riveting history at play here. Godfather tries his usual pre-match spiel offering Undertaker his ho's, noting that while he may be the 'Deadman', "I know that not everything is dead." Taker is offended so beats the hell out of Godfather, not to mention a battery of referees. Then the lights go out and we see Kane in the rafters as the show goes off the air. Okay, one to you, Cole.
Final Rating: N/R

THE HEAT RECAP:

Most Entertaining: The Hardy Boyz. They looked good in their brief showing against LOD, and hell, they beat them! A big night for the young duo.

Least Entertaining: Shane McMahon. He is finding new and exciting ways to ruin this show.

Quote of the Night: "I know you man, I've known you for a long time, and I know that you like ho's" - The Godfather to The Undertaker. The first and second parts are true, the third part...?

Match of the Night: The Hardy Boyz vs. LOD

Summary: Rotten. The matches were all incredibly short as to make room for Shane McMahon's self-indulgent promo. The one real angle - which was the Terri and Val Venis pregnancy stuff - was also a complete and utter joke. Tasteless, horrid, typical Attitude Era nonsense. As should be apparent by

now, *Heat* is a consistently dreadful show.
Verdict: 11

11.08.98 by James Dixon
Venue: Dallas, TX
Taped: 11.03.98
TV Rating: 4.2

Too Much vs. Bob Holly & Scorpio
Before we even get going, Scott Taylor gets on the mic and wants to address the crowd with a serious announcement: he loves Brian Christopher. Well, sure, what else is new? Al Snow wants to talk as well, because everyone in the Attitude Era has to gab on endlessly. As if it would be a crime if every thought they had didn't tumble out of their mouths. Al introduces Bob Holly and Scorpio, two guys sick of getting the stick and not the carrot, apparently. Yes, the debut of the J.O.B. Squad folks, another momentous moment right here on *Heat*. As ever it is brief, and for an extra kick in the nuts there is a botched finish to boot. With Scorp sent shitcanned to the outside, Too Much hook up Holly for their elevated Tennessee Jam double team finisher, but Al escapes and rolls up Taylor for the win. The mistake comes from the referee, who counts two and then just stops as if frozen in time, before slamming down his hand for a three. Either he forgot the finish or he was expecting Christopher to do something other than just standing on the top rope looking like a complete frigging imbecile, doing sod all as his partner got pinned. Woeful incompetence all around.
Final Rating: ½*

Backstage, Kevin Kelly interviews Val Venis and tells him people think he was insensitive in his handling of Terri's pregnancy. Val says it is because Terri is a manipulator and a liar, which Kelly questions. "I had a vasectomy!" explains Venis. Well, there you have it.

X-Pac vs. Steven Regal
Regal has changed his look and music, and now strongly resembles The Undertaker... Turns out it is the real Undertaker, who had decided to crash the party and prevent this match from happening. Pac warns Taker to get his TV time somewhere else rather than during his matches, so he gets his ass kicked. Couldn't they have done that during a match scheduled to feature worse wrestlers? I'm sure there are plenty of better choices on this show...

Marc Mero vs. The Godfather
...Like this one for instance! This would have been a pretty damn good choice for Undertaker to ruin. The match means nothing, it is only happening because it marks the refereeing debut of Shane McMahon. Though, that is not actually true. Before Shane was an overbearing TV character, he was a referee briefly a few years ago. Godfather gets on the mic and says that since Shane "will be running this place one day", he will hook him up with some skanks later on. He also says that given Mero's luck with women, he is getting jack. Vince and his Stooges watch the match backstage and discuss demoting Shane to being part of the ring crew if he flubs. This whole storyline would be better if the reason Shane was being punished was for his horrible commentary earlier in the year. The match might as well not happen, because it is all Shane storyline and nothing more. It is also lampooned by Vince and his goons talking over the top of the announcers, though that means no Michael Cole so, y'know, great! After they sleepwalk through some standard spots, Godfather scores the win on the soon to be departing Mero with the Pimp Drop. Next.
Final Rating: ½*

Next, a "training video" that only exists to show Sable bending over, thrusting, grunting and jiggling around. It would have been more subtle if she had just whipped out her enormous rubber cans and twisted her teats into the camera for five minutes. It is so blatant and gratuitous that you have to laugh.

Backstage, X-Pac says he might not be able to beat Undertaker, but he is going to fight him on *Raw* tomorrow night because he never backs down. That could almost be a cheesy gimmick for somebody...

The Outlaws come out for a promo, and after their usual pre-match catchphrases, get cut off by Vince. In full Dr. Evil mode, he tells them that they will be in a triple threat tag title defence at *Survivor Series* next week. That he follows up by naming their opponents as The Headbangers and D'Lo Brown & Mark Henry causes Billy Gunn to laugh his ass off rather than show any concern.

Jeff Jarrett vs. Droz

The recently "retired" Owen Hart joins us for commentary here, and as ever claims he is not the Blue Blazer. Didn't we already do this match in August? It doesn't need a second go around, that much I do know. We get a minute or two of generic clubbering before Hawk does a run in and attacks Droz. Animal sides with Droz and beats up Hawk, then the new look LOD drill him with the Doomsday Device in the ultimate final act of humiliation for Hawk. In just over a week he will try and kill himself by jumping off the Titantron as a result of his shame. The match was nothing, nothing at all.
Final Rating: ¼*

Promo Time: The Rock

As it stands, Rock is currently expelled from the *Survivor Series* tournament for the WWF Title because he pissed off Vince. He calls out McMahon right away, who has no problem responding. He repeats his same promo from *Raw*, saying his problem with Rock is down to his problem with "the people". Vince makes a match between Rock and Mark Henry tomorrow on *Raw*, one which Rock has to win if he wants to keep his job, but that will get him back into *Survivor Series* if he comes through it. Spoiler alert: Rock wins. Double spoiler alert: It was a ruse all along.

THE HEAT RECAP:

Most Entertaining: Billy Gunn, for rightly laughing at the prospects of his useless *Survivor Series* opponents

Least Entertaining: Brian Christopher, for standing on the top rope and watching his partner get beat like an utter clown.

Quote of the Night: "The Rock would much rather be the people's ass than ever kiss yours" - Rock to Vince. He sure changes his mind quickly. A week later he aligns with Vince as the new flag bearer for the Corporation

Match of the Night: Nothing doing.

Summary: Pointless. Nothing happened! The matches were bad, the promos were incredibly brief and led nowhere, and the show was filled with hype videos. It is amazing that the WWF is able to fill *Heat* with an hour of nothing, yet from 1993-1996 they presented *Raw* with the same run time and were consistently able to make it good. Cut out the crap and let guys wrestle, let the angles evolve and breath. We don't need to see two minute squash matches, because they do little for anybody involved. I cannot wait for this book to be over.

Verdict: 16

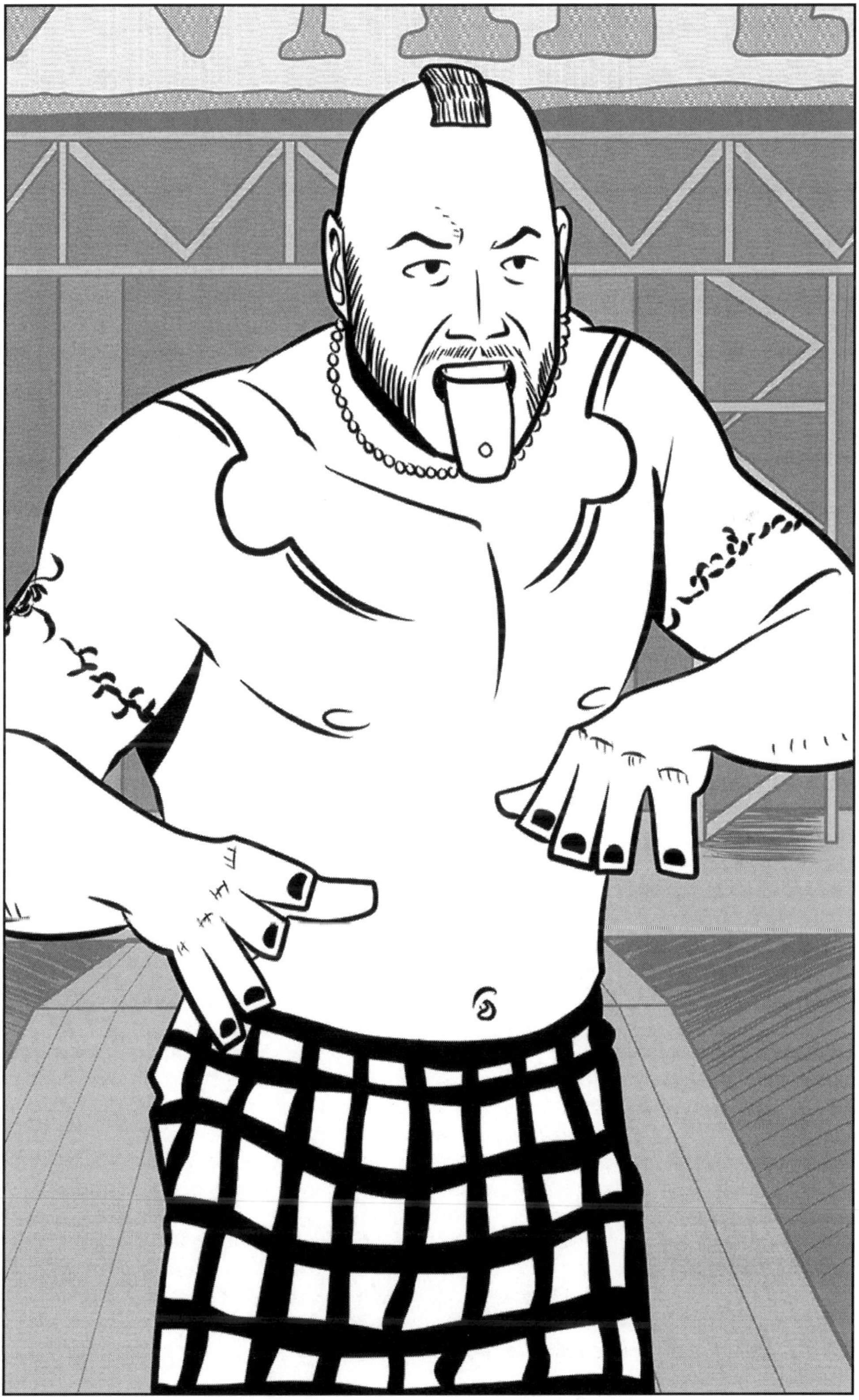

11.15.98 by James Dixon
Venue: St. Louis, MO
Taped: 11.15.98
TV Rating: 3.9

For the second time this month we are live, with this show coming before a rowdy sell out crowd in St. Louis prior to *Survivor Series: Deadly Game*. With literally all of the big stars competing on the PPV, I worry that it will be slimmer pickings than usual tonight. Jim Cornette hosts with Michael Cole.

The Legion of Doom vs. Bob Holly & Scorpio
The LOD are now heels for the first time in their WWF run, though they are less bad guys and more just "bad" by this stage. Scorpio and Holly, with Al Snow in tow, are collectively the J.O.B Squad now, a band of misfits who have banded together due to frustration at never winning. Naturally they won last time out, and they win again here as LOD's incredible run of defeats on *Heat* continues. Even a red hot crowd doesn't save this one, with LOD failing to win after the Doomsday Device and Snow clocking Droz with Head for the non-jobbing jobbers' win.
Final Rating: ½*

Tiger Ali Singh vs. Val Venis
Just when you thought *Heat* couldn't be more of a kick in the crotch, here comes Tiger Ali Singh to make things infinitely worse. We can be at least thankful that he doesn't get to speak, with Val's music cutting him off. Sadly Val does get to speak, and his trashy verbiage of choice results in a pained sigh from commentator Jim Cornette. I'm right there with you, Jim. Tiger is as adept as ever - that is to say completely and utterly useless, but Val still needs help to get the job done. He is aided in victory by his likeminded ally The Godfather, who charges to ringside and throws Singh into a ring post. Sort of. Tiger only skims it with his shoulder at best. Val finishes things with the fisherman suplex in short order. Another completely worthless match.
Final Rating: ¼*

After a long hype video for the PPV, DOA head to the ring! Oh come on, please Wrestling Gods, spare me another tedious Harris twins match...

...And then manna from Heaven! The debuting (as yet unnamed) Acolytes! They jump DOA pre-bell and pre-opponents, then beat the living hell out of them with chairs and stairs, before powerbombing Paul Ellering for good measure. "Bradshaw and Faarooq, together?" repeats Cole ad nauseum. Yes! Bradshaw. And Faarooq. Together. Jeez!

Backstage, the Headbangers jump the Outlaws during a promo, then Mark Henry and D'Lo Brown turn up to get involved in the fracas. Everyone is very tetchy this evening.

Promo Time: Sable
What the Wrestling Gods giveth, the Wrestling Gods taketh away. Spared a DOA match? Have a Sable promo instead! They are the only things of the era comparable to each other on the sheer horror scale. She guarantees victory in her title match with Jacqueline later tonight, prompting the arrival of Marc Mero. He warns Sable that she is going to get hurt by Jacqueline, who promptly sneaks up from behind and decks her in the back of the head with her title belt. I get that they were trying to hype the Women's title match, but nobody cares, they just want puppies.

Steve Blackman vs. Gangrel
By *Heat* standards this is a marathon match, clocking in at just over three minutes. Rather than slow things slightly as a result, they decide to take the

opposite approach and go at it with a pace and fury that I didn't expect at all. Thus a bout that looked pretty drab on paper turns out far better than I would have imagined. They slug it out as Michael Cole offers his picks for the tournament later, as if anyone cares a damn about his worthless uneducated opinions. With Blackman mounting a head of steam, Christian runs the distraction and Edge hits a missile dropkick, allowing Gangrel to hit the Impaler for the win. "Give the assist to Edge," says Cole, throwing in his current favourite announce tic of the month.

Final Rating: **¼

And this is where things become very uncomfortable to watch. Blue Blazer rappels from the ceiling, but he suffers a malfunction and gets stuck in the harness, becoming a human piñata for an irked Blackman. As an angle it is fairly cute, but given what happened to Owen Hart in this very same state some six months later when the WWF tried to run the same play again, all of the entertainment factor is taken out of it on retrospective viewing.

Promo Time: Vince McMahon

Vince has something to get off his chest regarding The Rock, his temporary replacement feud since the Steve Austin program began to jump the shark and run out of steam thanks to horrible booking that brought Undertaker and Kane into the fold. It was fine at first, but it peaked at *SummerSlam* and the last two pay-per-views have sucked as a result of their involvement. Rock being injected into the mix freshens things up significantly. Vince calls out Rock and his son Shane, the "lowly referee", and then Austin himself so he can vent his spleen. Just as he is about to talk, Undertaker comes down to stick his oar in. Austin can't be bothered to sit through his entrance so jumps Taker, as a three way brawl goes down in the ring. It soon becomes an all-out melee when X-Pac, Big Bossman, Mankind and Goldust get involved. Hell, even Steven Regal - complete with hard hat - hops in for a rumble. It is utter bedlam, and hot damn, what a highly effective and entertaining way to hard sell the imminent pay-per-view. During the chaos the lights go out and Kane arrives, which draws a huge pop, and he faces off with *Survivor Series* opponent Undertaker as we go off the air. A breathless, tremendously exciting segment.

THE HEAT RECAP:

Most Entertaining: The APA for saving us from a DOA match

Least Entertaining: Tiger Ali Singh. The second default option after standard choice DOA.

Quote of the Night: "You are no wrestler, you never will be a wrestler" - Marc Mero to Sable. Amen to that.

Match of the Night: Gangrel vs. Steve Blackman. It was good! Honestly.

Summary: The first half of the show was a disaster, but it really picked up at the end with the solid Blackman-Gangrel effort and the tremendous go-home brawl. The hot crowd, who popped for everyone and everything, also made this feel like a much bigger deal than the usual broadcast. That vibrancy makes the show feel important, and thus even during the pointless segments nothing drags. Still the same old problem of too many matches though, but at least stuff happened this week. An improvement for sure.

Verdict: 37

11.22.98 by James Dixon
Venue: Columbus, OH
Taped: 11.17.98
TV Rating: 4.1

After a couple of live shows recently, this was taped two nights after *Survivor Series*, prior to the 11/23 *Raw*.

Promo Time: The Corporation
The big hitters are out here for the opening segment, which makes it feel more like *Raw* and thus actually important. It certainly beats the pants off another drab Val Venis quickie bout. Vince reveals that Rock will defend his title against Mankind at *Rock Bottom*, and that Steve Austin will never again get a WWF Title shot. This will prove to be a lie. Out of kindness, Vince says Austin will be in the upcoming *Royal Rumble* if he can defeat The Undertaker at *Rock Bottom* in a Buried Alive Match. He does, in a really drastically crap encounter. Vince rides out some loud "asshole" chants and says that to prove he always does things for the fans (ha), he will appoint a new "free thinking" commissioner on *Raw*. It turns out to be Shawn Michaels, returning for his first regular on camera role since *WrestleMania XIV*. This was a more noteworthy opening than usual because it actually advanced storylines a little, but having Rock just stand there and not speak at all seems like a bit of a waste.

Michael Cole and Jim Ross reveal that Steve Austin "blacked out" after a match in San Jose "earlier today". Hmm. This show was filmed on November 17th, and the San Jose card took place on November 22nd... Now, that's in the future, isn't it? Okay, granted that was the air date for this show, but it is still interesting looking back at how they used to do things.

Too Much vs. The Hardy Boyz
The Hardys don't get an entrance because they are not yet over, which is probably down to their technicolour pants. They are so loud, Randy Savage circa 1992 would cringe. To my utter horror, the sickening sight of Jackyl appears on the screen, and to make it even worse he picks up a headset. No! Don't you dare let him talk! Thankfully all he says is: "Let me introduce, the Acolytes". Cue the arrival of the newly formed duo, who beat up everyone in sight just for the hell of it. Last week I commended them from saving me the revulsion of sitting through a DOA match, but this week I am somewhat less enthused. This match had potential to be fairly good! Couldn't they have waited for something worse?
Final Rating: N/R

Road agent one-eyed Jack (Lanza) gets on the phone from San Jose and gives us an update on Steve Austin. Lanza says Austin has been struggling all week, and Michael Cole adds context by claiming the Undertaker belting him with a shovel on *Raw* was responsible. I actually appreciate the effort and planning that has gone into this little angle, as well on that note as the foresight in debuting the Acolytes as a standalone unit prior to them becoming part of the Undertaker's upcoming Ministry of Darkness. Backstage, the Stooges tell Vince about Steve Austin's situation, but he is far less pleased than you might expect. JR says it is because McMahon - despite their differences - realises Austin is a massive box office attraction, which he is, but if that is the reason why has Vince been trying to get him out of the WWF all year? There are some logic gaps there.

Gangrel vs. Al Snow
After Gangrel's fun outing last week, I am rather looking forward to this. Al Snow, another *Heat* regular of late,

doesn't disappoint by throwing in a German suplex just seconds in. The vampire responds with a double underhook suplex and Snow comes back with a wheelbarrow variant, as I begin to suspect they are participating in a private wager to see who can hit the most suplexes. Much shenanigans occur from the J.O.B. Squad and the Brood, leading to a double disqualification. What a shame, that was shaping up to be fun before the copout finish.

Final Rating: *¼

We then get footage from *Raw* and Hawk's ridiculous though perversely entertaining suicide attempt, before heading to the locker room where Kevin Kelly catches up with Droz and Animal. Animal is still too emotional about the whole ordeal to offer anything, so Droz steps in. He says the old LOD would dwell on the past, but the new LOD won't do that, then does a pretty damn good Hawk rip-off promo. Animal still doesn't say anything, he just walks off. Hell, I like this angle. Droz as the enabler, the trouble causer and the man responsible for pushing Hawk off the Titantron was a good twist! It had depth, layers, and even logic. Droz wanted the spot, so he preyed on Hawk's weaknesses and used them to rip the bonds of friendship and camaraderie apart. It is devious heeldom at its best. It's a shame the future writing went nowhere with the storyline, because there was something there, I really think that. I realise I am in the overwhelming minority on this one.

Marc Mero vs. The Big Bossman
This is a strange match-up given that both guys are heels. Bossman is bigger and more heelish due to his Corporation leanings, so Mero plays the nominal babyface role. The state of his almost-finished WWF career is brought into sharp focus here when he jobs to a Bossman Slam in record time after miscommunication with Jacqueline, who accidentally tripped him thinking he was Bossman. Post match, Mero calls Jacqui out for having failed to get the job done with Sable and then fires her. Another angle on *Heat*!
Final Rating: SQUASH (Not rated)

Promo Time: Mankind
Poor Mankind is suffering emotionally from the cruel rejection of "dad", Vince McMahon at *Survivor Series*, and is out here to vent. He heads out with a leaf-blower wrapped in a bow, which he had intended as a present for Vince. He outlines in some detail how that won't be happening (see *The Heat Recap*), and announces his "divorce" from the corporate family. Mankind says he can forgive everything that Vince did to him, apart from being forced to wear nice dress shoes. So furious is Mick with the shoes that he throws them into the crowd. Mankind asks the question on everyone's lips: where is Mr. Socko? It turns out he is wearing him on his foot, and he promises to keep him there until he gets chance to ram it down Vince's throat. The crowd love that, but the McMahons don't, so appear in the aisle to counter. "On behalf of the McMahon family, I would like for you to understand one thing Mick: and that is that you are a living, breathing personification of the fact that you can't shine shit". Zing! Helluva way to counter! Vince reminds Mick that love hurts, and he is going to prove as much by putting him in a triple threat match on *Raw* for the Hardcore Title with the Big Bossman and Ken Shamrock. With a wicked sneer and a condescending wave, Vince leaves Mick with the words, "have a nice day," as Mankind's "at peace" theme tinkles away in the background. This entire thing, from start to finish, was glorious. Mick was great, with McMahon at his absolute deplorable bastard best. Exchanges like these are what made

Mick Foley into an underdog hero with the Federation faithful, leading to his epic WWF Title win two months later. What a goddamn great segment to appear on *Heat*. In fact, I would go out on a limb and say it is the best *ever* segment to appear on the show to date by a mile.

Jeff Jarrett vs. Kurrgan

Sable is out here to do commentary, clad in full-on inappropriate bondage gear. Is there a worse role for her? Her weakest asset is her scratching voice; why would you make her talk? At least we get the guilty delight of seeing Kurrgan work a singles match, and since I last saw him he has added a seizure helmet to go with his tie-dye shirt. The contrast from this time last year when Kurrgan - as the Interrogator in the Truth Commission - was demolishing everyone in his path is remarkable. With the referee distracted dealing with an Oddities-ICP fracas entirely unrelated to the in-ring action, Debra distracts Kurrgan with her big fake waps. He dances in response, and Jarrett clocks him with a guitar to the head for the win. I hate finishes like that. Why was the referee concerning himself with such matters? If there was a brawl in the crowd at a football match, would the referee interject himself and leave the players on the pitch to it? Post match, Sable is cross with Debra and lets her know about it, setting up a feud between them which goes nowhere.
Final Rating: ½*

After the usual awful Val Venis promo, we go back to Blackjack Lanza on the phone. He doesn't offer a great deal more insight into the Austin situation other than confirming that 'Stone Cold' blames Undertaker.

WWF Intercontinental Championship
Ken Shamrock (c) vs. Val Venis

The perceived importance of tonight's show continues to increase by playing host to a title match, it's just a shame Val Venis is wrestling again. I was never particularly moved by him one way or another prior to this book, but his samey matches, repetitive gimmick and corny promos have really soured me on him of late. There is precious little to talk about here, because the match is just two guys hitting bland moves in a basic bout that typifies "WWF Style". When Shamrock hooks the ankle lock, Mankind charges down for the save with his leaf blower and that is a DQ. Big Bossman isn't far behind, and drills Mankind repeatedly with his nightstick. Then Shamrock joins in the fun, commandeering the leaf blower as we go off the air.
Final Rating: ½*

THE HEAT RECAP:

Most Entertaining: Mankind. A strong night for Mick Foley.

Least Entertaining: Jackyl. Everyone else was good tonight, and in truth Jackyl didn't do anything wrong here. It's just that the sight of him alone makes me see red.

Quote of the Night: "You see dad, I put this nice little bow on here because I was saving this leaf blower for father's day. So now, dad, when those leaves lay on the ground all winter long causing a detriment in the nitrogen level, and the subsequent decaying leaf matter causes a lack of oxidation to the soil, and your lawn becomes the laugh stock of Greenwich, don't blame me" - Mankind utters perhaps the strangest speech ever heard on WWF programming

Match of the Night: Gangrel vs. Al Snow

Summary: Good! I mean it is not great

or anything as the best match was barely over *, but the strong promos and angles carried this. For once, *Heat* felt like a big deal, like a show that mattered and affected the grand scheme of things. It makes a huge difference, and the strong fluff combined with star power makes it easy to forgive the criminally brief snippets of wrestling on offer.
Verdict: 48

11.29.98 By James Dixon
Venue: Philadelphia, PA
Taped: 11.29.98
TV Rating: ??

The show is live from the First Union Center in Philly, home of next year's *WrestleMania XV*. Quite remarkably, it is sold out to the tune of 20,000 people. It is an incredible testament to the current wave of success the WWF is enjoying that they can cram so many people in for a B-Show. They are also taping *Shotgun* and *Super Astros* tonight, none of which helps explain why so many people felt compelled to attend. The reality is Steve Austin, who is headlining with The Rock, The Undertaker and Kane in a four way for the title. Still though, a *WrestleMania* sized crowd for *Heat* is quite a thing to behold. Will the WWF reward their audience with long, hard-fought matches and important happenings? I am not holding my breath.

Christian vs. Duane Gill
If this was a few years ago on *Raw* it would be a squash match, thanks to Gills then-status as enhancement talent. Now, he is the Light Heavyweight Champion thanks to his association with the J.O.B. Squad. Cornette calls his reign as champion a farce, which it is, and rightly points out that it kills the prestige of the title. It never recovers. They work a generic bout for a minute or two before the Blue Meanie makes his surprise debut from the crowd, resulting in a mass Brood-Jobbers brawl and the match getting thrown out. Given the names involved, no doubt it will come as a shock that the crowd was well into all of this.
Final Rating: ¾*

D'Lo Brown vs. Steve Blackman
You have to give credit to this crowd, they are certainly up for having a good time here regardless of what crap the WWF tries to feed them tonight. They rail on D'Lo, absolutely barracking him with a chorus of boos and loud chants of "D'Lo sucks". I mean, they don't go as far as actually popping for Blackman or anything, but they are invested. The match is similar to the first, going all of a minute or two before they brawl awkwardly on the outside waiting for Owen Hart to appear in his Blue Blazer garb. In keeping with his recent theme of making an ass of himself, he gets his cape stuck on the ring apron, allowing Blackman to pound on him repeatedly just like last week. Unfortunately, our Steve is not so bright, and forgets that he is supposed to be wrestling a match. He gets counted out due to his obsession with kicking the Blazer's ass, for our second consecutive cheap finish. Let's see how long this hot crowd stays hot if they keep getting fed rot like this.
Final Rating: ½*

Backstage, Kevin Kelly is with the Oddities. Luna does the talking (and snarling), challenging the Headbangers and ICP to an eight-person tag match. That doesn't happen, unfortunately. Yes, unfortunately! I think it would have been a lot of fun.

The Headbangers vs. Supply & Demand
Oh good, more Val Venis. No skanks for the 'Bangers tonight, because Val kept them up all night yesterday apparently. Godfather needs to get himself some

more durable ho's. Val starts into his pre-match promo, noticing the Headbangers "skirts" and growling, "Hello ladies". That gets him jumped, then a minute later the Oddities arrive at ringside. Outside interference for the third match in a row? Sure, it's Attitude, let's throw booking sensibility out of the window. The inevitable occurs a moment later, and the 'Bangers do the job courtesy of the distraction. It grows very tiresome. Why do the Oddities still use an ICP track as their entrance theme if they are so at odds with them?
Final Rating: ¾*

In Vince McMahon's sky box, the Outlaws arrive for a cordial meeting. They are all smiles. Vince wants to talk business, seemingly about to offer them a spot in the Corporation. It stems from a situation on *Raw* where the duo aided the Corporation in battering the J.O.B. Squad, though it all turns out to be a big fat bait and switch when it plays out further on *Raw*. For a change.

WWF European Championship
X-Pac (c) vs. Mark Henry

Before we begin, Henry recites a dreadful poem about Chyna, then gets distracted by an indiscreetly planted issue of *Raw Magazine* featuring Chyna on the cover. X-Pac takes advantage early on, and every time Henry mounts a head of steam he gets sidetracked. The lack of focus costs him the match, with Pac jumping off the top with an X-Factor for the win. That was super short. Afterwards, Pac warns Henry that if he gets out of line with Chyna he will suffer, then reacts with disgust to his DX brethren the Outlaws hobnobbing with the Corporation.
Final Rating: ¾*

We go to comments from Steve Austin filmed at yesterday's house show in Boston, and he is furious with Vince McMahon refusing to let him wrestle on TV without clearance. Undertaker chimes in next with a pre-recorded promo of his own. He tells Austin to come and find him tomorrow on *Raw* so he can sacrifice his soul to the Ministry of Darkness. Deep. Paul Bearer has a similar warning for Kane, telling him that if he turns up tomorrow he will be carted away in a straightjacket. This was fluff.

Jeff Jarrett vs. Kane

The pop for Kane is ridiculous. This is actually a pretty big match for *Heat*, with both guys among the upper echelon of stars. Kane is as hot as he has ever been and Jarrett is on a definite rise as the new-look "don't piss me off" version of his character. The bout is hardly an epic though, going a shade over two minutes before Debra gets in the ring for a distraction. Kane decides to chokeslam her so Jarrett belts him with his guitar for the DQ. Kane completely no sells it, so Jarrett does the smart thing and bails. All action for the duration, but too brief as ever.
Final Rating: *

The Big Bossman & Ken Shamrock
vs. Mankind & Al Snow

The Rock heads out for this to join the commentary team, and he gets an enormous pop as well, despite his status as supposed leading heel. Hell, everyone is over on this show. The characters were all strong, even if the wrestling was severely lacking in places. They waste little time getting right into things, with Snow especially looking psyched to be involved in a high profile bout like this. The action is good, with the short time remaining resulting in the guys going for it, but unfortunately for them it is overshadowed by the sheer presence of The Rock. It is merely a vehicle to promote Rock-Mankind at *Rock Bottom*, and we get a preview of that when Mankind launches himself at Rock for the two to engage in an arena-wide brawl. Bossman pins

Snow in the ring, which hardly matters, then things get really excitable when the J.O.B. Squad and The Brood invade the ring to finish what they started earlier. Whew. A fine, wild and unpredictable end to an otherwise nothing show.
Final Rating: *½

THE HEAT RECAP:

Most Entertaining: Kane. I usually groan at the sight of him, certainly as time has gone on that is more true than ever, but he looked like a star tonight. Hell, he even put some effort in!

Least Entertaining: Duane Gill. I get that this is Attitude, I know that titles don't mean anything, but the sight of Gill with that Light Heavyweight title is a joke.

Quote of the Night: "He doesn't even work here, he is some joker from ECW," rants Jim Cornette of the Blue Meanie. Quite.

Match of the Night: The Big Bossman & Ken Shamrock vs. Mankind & Al Snow

Summary: A wasted opportunity. With 20,000 rabid fans packed into the building, the WWF had an opportunity to put on a spectacle that would make *Heat* must-see viewing. Instead they delivered the same underwhelming show, devoid of important matches or angles, or anything that fans would need to tune in for. It is the same old Russo story: more is more. Why not two matches, both of them long and competitive, then an angle or two that lead somewhere thrown in. Who gets over with these two minute matches? What do they achieve. It is a waste of time and resources, and certainly a waste of a damn good crowd who deserved better.
Verdict: 20

12.06.98 by Arnold Furious
Venue: Baltimore, MD
Taped: 11.30.98
TV Rating: 4.1

We're in Baltimore, Maryland. This was taped after *Raw* the week beforehand. Hosts are Kevin Kelly and Jim Cornette, which is the best possible team the WWF could have dug up for a B-show. Naturally, this won't last.

WWF Light Heavyweight Championship
Duane Gill (c) vs. Taka Michinoku
This being the WWF, the Light Heavyweight title is now a total joke, having lasted as a division for all of a year. Gill is pre-Gillberg and needs the J.O.B. Squad to get him over. Gill would actually hold this belt until February 2000 when the WWF remembered he still had it and needed a prop to help Essa Rios get over. Taka dominates the whole match until he goes for the Michinoku Driver and Gill inside cradles him to retain the title CLEAN. The Acolytes run in to destroy Kaientai after the match. This is before the Acolytes had joined with the Undertaker and they're being managed by Don Callis, aka the Jackyl, which rather explains the name. Callis would get fired, the Acolytes joined with Taker, and the rest is history.
Final Rating: *

Video Control shows Steve Austin arriving before throwing to "Bop It" with Michael Cole and Grandmasta Robbie. Super fans George and Adam and the Oddities join in the fun. I'm not entirely sure what the hell Bop It is, but this was an advert for it. A bad one.

The Legion of Doom vs. Too Much
Too Much are playing the role of cruiserweight jobbers. Droz takes the knee and makes Scott Taylor tap out to

a half crab, which is fairly brutal looking. Animal doesn't seem to care that Droz tortures the poor kid long after the bell, and naturally the crowd don't care either because Too Much are heels.
Final Rating: ½*

Video Control brings us some Steve Austin antics from backstage. He's bought a ticket and will be ringside drinking beers. Quite why he's backstage if he bought a ticket is anyone's guess. Can't he just come out and sit at ringside anyway? Why does he need a ticket? Elsewhere Taylor is attended to by a doctor. He's got an injured knee. This was to cover for an actual injury he'd already sustained.

Promo Time: Owen Hart.
He's got a blockbuster announcement about the Blue Blazer. Crowd do not care for that. He announces he'll be coming out of retirement to face Steve Blackman at *Rock Bottom* to defend the honour of the Blue Blazer. Every Owen/Blazer segment is downright depressing when viewed with the benefit of hindsight.

The Rock, The Big Bossman & Ken Shamrock vs. Gangrel, Edge & Christian
WWF Champion The Rock gives this one more than a little star power, and the Brood are over on entrance alone. Shame the match is taking place on *Heat* where nothing and nobody get any time to tell a story. I'd love to see a real Edge-Shamrock series; the snippets here are really good. Rock dominates whenever he's in there as none of the Brood are anywhere near his level. We get some fun back-and-forth until DX run in for the DQ after about four minutes. The Outlaws were defending their tag belts against Bossman & Shamrock at the following *Rock Bottom* PPV.
Final Rating: **

Mark Henry vs. Jeff Jarrett
This is right after Mark Henry's date with Chyna. Henry dominates with power for the entire minute of the match until Jarrett grabs "El Kabong" (his guitar) only for D'Lo Brown to steal it and bash Jeff over the head for the DQ. Goldust comes out afterwards to challenge Jarrett to a striptease match. If Goldust loses, he strips, if Jarrett loses, Debra strips. That's another match for the *Rock Bottom* show. **Final Rating:** ¼*

Kurrgan & Luna Vachon vs. Tiger Ali Singh & Babu
Yes, Kurrgan and Luna, believe it or not. The match practically screams filler. Babu is absolutely worthless, yet he's the "talented" one on his team. Luna beats the crap out of Babu and its declared a no contest. The only good thing about this is that Singh never tagged in.
Final Rating: Pointless

Mankind vs. The Undertaker
This is the big main event, it's the second last Foley-Taker bout and it has a big match atmosphere. It feels like a blow-off match to a feud that dates back over two years. That is until Steve Austin finally arrives to take his ringside seat as part of the build for his Buried Alive match with Taker. Unfortunately, this one kicks off just five minutes before the show finishes. It borders on a hardcore match and has a lot of brawling in it, though Earl Hebner stops the line being crossed too far. Mankind kicks Taker in the balls to block the chokeslam but Rock runs in for the DQ, and Austin sees the opportunity to give Taker a beating. The show ends with all four brawling to sell the dreadful *Rock Bottom* PPV.
Final Rating: *¾

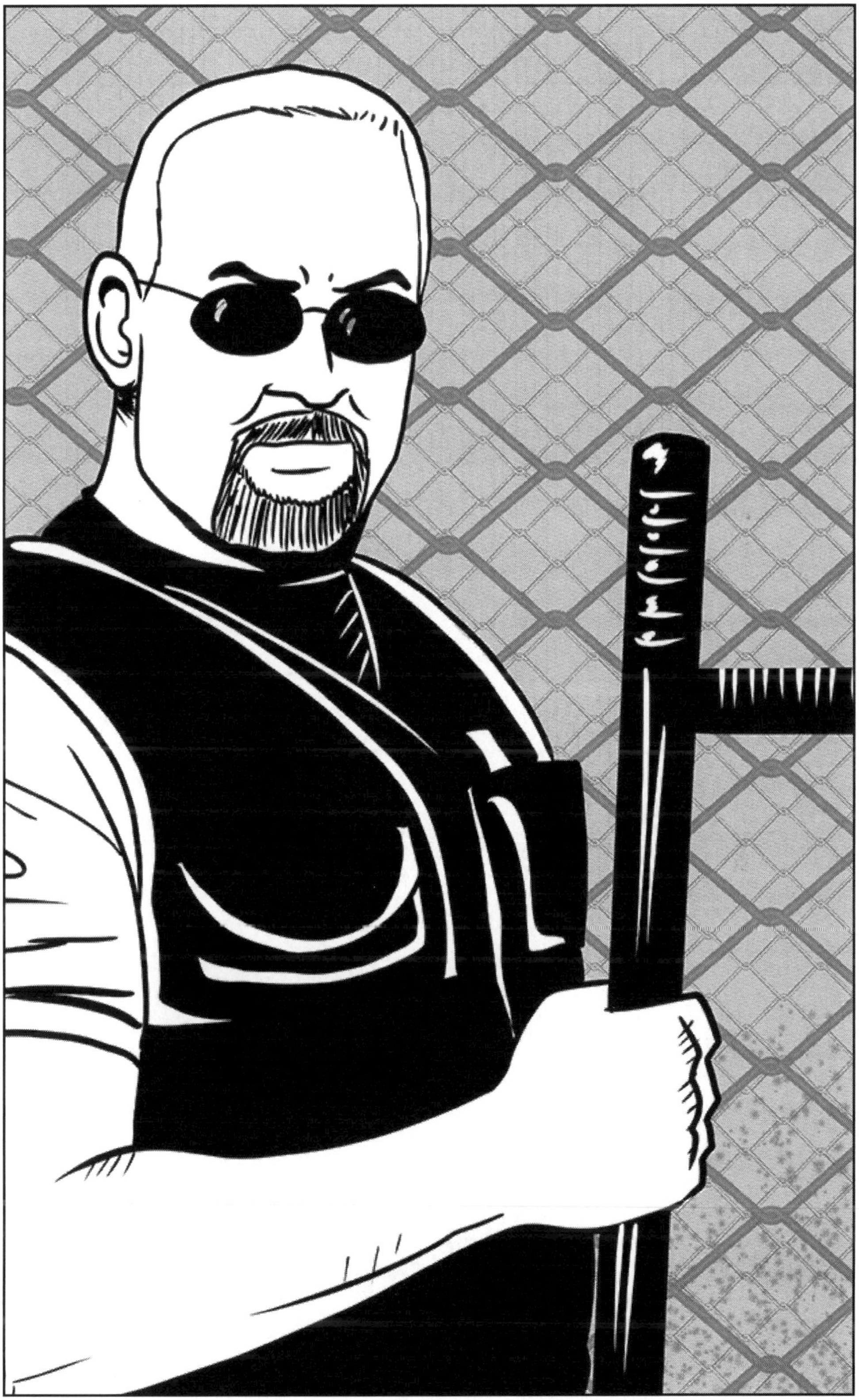

THE HEAT RECAP:

Most Entertaining: The Rock

Least Entertaining: Tiger Ali Singh

Quote of the Night: "Take your little microphone and get the hell outta here. I've got things to do" – Steve Austin puts Michael Cole in his place.

Match of the Night: The Corporation vs. The Brood

Summary: Despite all of the star power, this was a bad show. In forty five minutes they just tried to cram too much in. Nothing had time to develop. Six matches inside of an hour is just way too many. Frankly, I question the need for the Oddities match or the LOD match or the Jarrett match. Clip those three out and give half the show to the Corporation-Brood contest and a quarter to Taker and Mankind. That would be a good show. This was a bunch of unmemorable stuff happening, one thing after another. Lots of "appearance" pops for the top guys but no substance.
Verdict: 21

12.13.98 by Arnold Furious
Venue: Vancouver, BC
Taped: 12.13.98
TV Rating: 3.8

This is the pre-show for the *Rock Bottom* PPV. We're in Vancouver, British Columbia. Hosts are Kevin Kelly and Shane McMahon.

Promo Time: Vince McMahon
He tells us there's no chance in hell that Steve Austin will win the WWF Title again. Tonight Austin can qualify for the *Royal Rumble* by beating the Undertaker in the Buried Alive match. Vince dedicates the PPV to The Rock, the "best champion there has ever been," before unveiling two enormous posters with The Rock on them. Vince goes for the cheap heat jugular by running down Canada and telling the fans to beg to become American and renounce their citizenship. It might be cheap heat but it is magnificent. He brings out Shane McMahon, who'll be on commentary tonight.

WWF Light Heavyweight Championship:
Duane Gill (c) vs. Matt Hardy
Matt has to work slightly heel against the underdog champion. Splash Mountain should finish. Quebrada should finish. Matt doesn't go for the pin and in comes the recently debuted Blue Meanie to DDT Matt and allow Gill to retain his title.
Final Rating: *

Promo Time: Mankind
He has a contract that states if the injured Rock can't compete tonight he gets the title given to him. He offers to erase that clause if Vince McMahon gives him what he wants. This was just here to sell storyline going into the PPV.

Brian Christopher vs. Kevin Quinn
Scotty is in Brian's corner on crutches after last week's abuse from Droz. Scott would miss six weeks of action so Christopher gets to wrestle in singles. Taylor joins commentary so Shane can insinuate he's gay. Quinn isn't the best of cruiserweights but he throws himself into the bumps to compensate for it. They botch the finish when Quinn fails to grab a roll up and instead FACEPLANTS a bump. Even though it was supposed to be a roll up, Christopher still took the shock loss. "I thought you were pretty fly for a white guy, but I guess not" says Scotty as he leaves commentary. Proof there was life before Scotty 2 Hotty. Quinn would actually team with Christopher a few times before Taylor took offence and

waffled him with a crutch.
Final Rating: *¾

Triple H vs. Droz

Seeing as Hunter isn't on the PPV, something that will probably boggle anyone's mind who only knows Triple H as a big star, he's working Droz on *Heat*. Kelly tries to plug the PPV during this match, but it's so short he can only get half the shill in. Hunter channels Flair with a load of chops and bumps before finishing with the Pedigree inside two minutes. After the match Commissioner Shawn Michaels comes out to ban DX from ringside during the tag title match on the pay-per-view, and books the Outlaws into a "warm up match" on *Heat* as punishment for making him look foolish earlier in the week, when they rejected his advances regarding a spot in the Corporation.
Final Rating: ¾*

Video Control takes us to Vince McMahon, who's interviewed by his son, allowing him to actually not talk down to someone asking him questions. He promises he'll get to Mankind and we'll see the title match tonight. More storyline build that wouldn't pay off until the PPV itself.

Promo Time: Debra & Jeff Jarrett

This is to shill the striptease match for the PPV, trying to get a few extra buys from any horn-dogs watching on a Sunday evening. Debra's voice goes right through me. I'm not sure what she says, something about scarring the soul and burying humanity in its own excretion.

The New Age Outlaws vs. The Acolytes

Looks like Jackyl has been fired, as he's not here. The match is a thrashing for the Outlaws until Shamrock & Bossman run in for the DQ after two minutes, which makes NO SENSE AT ALL. Why would they want the match to end? Surely they want the Outlaws to take a longer beating? Meanwhile the Acolytes, pissed off about the DQ, beat Shamrock & Bossman down. That's the end of the show.
Final Rating: ½*

THE HEAT RECAP:

Most Entertaining: Vince McMahon

Least Entertaining: Shane McMahon. I hasn't missed him on commentary.

Quote of the Night: "You people here in Canada can't make up your mind, whether you want to be French or English. You can't speak either language very well". "The French hate the English... justifiably. The English hate the French, justifiably." – Vince McMahon rocks the cheap heat.

Match of the Night: Brian Christopher vs. Kevin Quinn. Even with the big botch at the end.

Summary: Being the PPV pre-show didn't really alter the rushed feel of the broadcast, nor lessen the sheer number of segments the WWF tried to cram into it. At least there were less matches, but the two missing bouts were replaced by two in-ring promos. Although one of those, the opening Vince McMahon one, was easily the most entertaining part of the show.
Verdict: 29

12.20.98 by Arnold Furious
Venue: Tacoma, WA
Taped: 12.14.98
TV Rating: 3.5

We're in Tacoma, Washington. Hosts are Kevin Kelly and Shane McMahon.

WWF European Championship
X-Pac (c) vs. Tiger Ali Singh

Who thought this was a good idea? Probably the same people who hired Tiger in the first place. Waltman can carry his end but Tiger looks so uncoordinated and out of place. Tiger takes ages to come out of the corner after the Broncobuster, leading to Waltman screaming "COME ON" at him. Eventually he gets the memo and runs into the X-Factor. For Tiger this wasn't all that bad. Waltman worked around him.
Final Rating: ¾*

Brian Christopher & Kevin Quinn vs. The Hardy Boyz

Quinn continues his slightly botchy style over from last week. Like a slow-motion rana. Unfortunately, Shane and Scotty spend the entire match talking about how "close" Too Much are as a tag team, continuing the implied gay connection. Thank god they dropped this storyline. Jeff actually hits the Swanton here, popping the crowd, only for Quinn to pop back up begging off. Considering this is the WWF, there's next to no selling in this. Quinn comes off the top and gets met with a Jeff dropkick, which is glorious. Matt even gets a moonsault in before Christopher hits the Tennessee Jam to win. This was barely over three minutes but absolutely tremendous. No selling of any kind, but the Hardys wrestled like their lives depended on it. Something the brawl-heavy Attitude Era didn't see very often.
Final Rating: **¾

Al Snow vs. Droz

Signs that Droz isn't good enough to be in the LOD #1: he's a jobber on *Heat*. Animal doesn't even bother staying out here to watch another failure of his new tag team partner. In his place comes Drunk Hawk, who clocks Droz with his broken arm cast - channelling Bob Orton Jr., from 1985 - and Snow wins with the Snow Plow. Hawk promises to reveal a the "dark secret" that he and Droz share on *Raw*.
Final Rating: ½*

The Headbangers vs. The Oddities

Kurrgan & Golga are competing but that's not the story, as the Oddities have an enormous Christmas present for the 'Bangers in a box at ringside. The match is just a momentary distraction. The Headbangers open their gift and it's George "The Animal" Steele, who beats them up for the DQ. Nobody cares about that though. Post match, Steele dances to the Oddities music and eats the turnbuckle.
Final Rating: ¼*

Promo Time: DX

Billy Gunn threatens to "jerk a knot" in Shawn Michaels' ass. I have no idea what that means, but basically the Outlaws are upset they lost the tag titles. Hunter cuts a promo about the debuting Test, saying DX break all the rules. This brings out The Rock to run DX down. "The Rock nearly put your bony ass in a coma" – of X-Pac. "You look like Tarzan and wrestle like Jane" – of Hunter. DX respond by making fun of Rock's pectoral surgery and laying down a challenge.

The New Age Outlaws vs. DOA

This is the kind of match that doesn't need any time, so it belongs on *Heat*. Minimal heat on Road Dogg, some boring DOA offence but only a bit, a hot tag and a typical Outlaw tag match condensed down to a bite-sized three minutes. The finish sees Paul Ellering miscue on a briefcase shot and Gunn scores the pin. This is how I like my DOA matches; short. DOA beat down Ellering for the screw up. Why do DOA have a briefcase anyway? Motorcycle gang business?
Final Rating: *½

Video Control gives us Mankind going

nuts backstage, singing Christmas carols with the wrong lyrics ("walking around in women's underwear") and smashing stuff up.

Mankind vs. The Rock vs. The Big Bossman vs. Ken Shamrock

This fatal four way match features three Corporate team members and Mankind, who they hate. However the odds are slightly improved by only two guys being in the match at any point. So they take it in turns to beat Mankind down. While this is going on we cut to Vince McMahon and Test watching backstage making comments like "that's gonna leave a mark". How did Test not get over with zingers like that? Mankind gets the Mandible Claw on Bossman so Vince strolls down to watch. Rock tags in blind, the numbers distract and the Rock Bottom on a chair sets up the Corporate Elbow. A typical nWo-esque numbers beat down on a top babyface. In a forgotten moment, Vince McMahon pulls out The Corporate Sock and locks Mankind in the Mandible Claw. DX run in for the save.
Final Rating: **

THE HEAT RECAP:

Most Entertaining: The Rock

Least Entertaining: Tiger Ali Singh

Quote of the Night: "The Rock sees that bony jabroni X-Pac, waving his arms around in the Corporate ring" – The Rock.

Match of the Night: The Hardy Boyz vs. Brian Christopher & Kevin Quinn

Summary: This might be my favourite episode of *Heat* so far. There were two decent matches, one featuring the Hardys showcasing themselves and working ten times harder than the guys on the regular roster. Also both The Rock and Vince McMahon were at their hilarious heel best. Even the likes of DOA and Tiger Ali Singh couldn't drag the show down. That's the mark of excellence. A rare thumbs up episode of *Heat*.
Verdict: 39

12.27.98 by Arnold Furious
Venue: Spokane, WA
Taped: 12.15.98
TV Rating: ??

We're in Spokane, Washington. This was actually taped two weeks ago. Hosts are Kevin Kelly and Shane McMahon.

Promo Time: Vince McMahon

He's here to introduce Kane. The 'Big Red Machine' had been sent to an insane asylum before Christmas, but now he's out as a member of the Corporation, as long as he does whatever Vince tells him to. Kane actually returned on the *Raw* that was taped the same day as this episode of *Heat*. Taping schedules; we hate them at the History of Wrestling offices. Vince runs down Kane's mental acumen and details his history and his "gargoyle-like Frankenstein face". "Sometimes, life's a bitch". After calling Kane a "mentally deficient freak," he points out that Kane is now *his* freak. Vince then threatens to send Kane back to that sanatorium until he dies. As is typical "opening talky bit" procedure, Vince books a match: Kane vs. X-Pac for his own personal amusement. "Thank you, Mr McMahon" says Robo-Kane. This show feels like a mini-*Raw*.

Video Control goes backstage with Vince McMahon ordering Kane to make him coffee. Hope he doesn't bump into Chris Jericho!

Mosh vs. Golga

George Steele is with the Oddities. He'll

even wrestle a match next week, though that's a story for another time. Golga squashes Mosh and would win with the Vertical Splash, but Thrasher grabs his leg. That brings George Steele charging in for the DQ.
Final Rating: ½*

Video Control takes us back to *Raw* on Monday where Mark Henry went off on one of his sexual adventures with Jacqueline and Terri. Shane cracks me up by calling Mark, "The Chocolate One", and almost breaks himself on the air.

Promo Time: PMS
Unfortunately Michael Cole is out here to do the interview with Terri Runnels and Jacqueline. Jacqui tells us PMS stands for "Pretty Mean Sisters" to kick the interview off. I never understood this gimmick. Terri says she feels disrespected so they'll be putting a few men in their place. The almost entirely male audience is not best pleased, until Jacqueline kicks Michael Cole in the bollocks. Even though that's a hard thing to botch they still manage it. Everything that I hate about Attitude in one segment. Where's the pay off for this? Cole vs. Jacqueline?

Jeff Jarrett & Owen Hart vs. Supply & Demand
One of the WWF's best teams, and indeed most underrated, in Jarrett & Hart. Supply & Demand was a short-lived team, which made sense. Val was a sex addict, Godfather was a pimp. I'm surprised they didn't keep them together longer to have Val drag Godfather up in the ring, because they're already popular as a unit here. Godfather offers Debra a spot as one of his ho's, which she rejects. I don't understand why they wasted so much time on Debra. One of Godfather's ho's here is better looking and has bigger tits. Debra can't be in the position she's in because of her mic skills. Val and Godfather are so much fun to watch as a team, while both Jarrett and Hart are brilliant bumpers and sellers. Unfortunately the match is only three minutes long, but it's all kinds of great. Should have been a PPV match at the bare minimum. Debra flashes Val the goods, which you'd think he'd be used to as a porn star, and Jarrett finishes with The Stroke. Cracking little tag contest. This team could have made Godfather. Shame it didn't last.
Final Rating: **½

WWF Tag Team Championship
Big Bossman & Ken Shamrock (c) vs. The Hardy Boyz
An early title opportunity for the Hardys. As per usual they make the most of their two minutes, with Jeff in particular looking good, bumping around for Shamrock. Bossman Slam puts Jeff down and Shamrock hooks the ankle lock on the unconscious youngster for good measure. The Acolytes run down to destroy the tag champs. You'd think they'd be next in line for the belts, but Jarrett and Hart won them instead.
Final Rating: *½

X-Pac vs. Kane
This is not for X-Pac's prestigious European Title. Commissioner Shawn Michaels boots DX from ringside to ensure that X-Pac has no chance. X-Pac tries to work the leg, but Kane doesn't sell anything so that doesn't really work, although it briefly stops him from throwing punches. X-Pac tries to work this like Shawn vs. Undertaker, only with more spin kicks. X-Factor barely gets two as X-Pac throws everything at Kane, but he's caught in a chokeslam. "BOOYAA" – Shane. That'll do it. The match is ninety seconds long, but showed X-Pac's tactics when battling a bigger opponent, condensed admittedly. DX save X-Pac from a Tombstone.

Final Rating: **

THE HEAT RECAP:

Most Entertaining: Vince McMahon

Least Entertaining: PMS

Quote of the Night: "Kane is both a certifiable lunatic as well as a certifiable idiot" – Vince McMahon, to Kane's face.

Match of the Night: Jeff Jarrett & Owen Hart vs. Val Venis & The Godfather

Summary: Another good *Heat* to end the year. It felt like a good quality, short episode of *Raw*, rather than a secondary show. When they booked *Heat* strong it worked as a quick show. It was almost like a night off for the wrestlers as they'd only work for two minutes and it all came across as energised and exciting. Having talent like Vince McMahon, Kane and DX on the show made it seem more important. Plus the guys who normally got screwed for spots could put themselves in the shop window by working their socks off opposite big talent.
Verdict: 39

TELEVISION CLASSICS

WHAT THE WORLD *WAS* WATCHING

***** MATCHES

****¾ MATCHES

****½ MATCHES

****¼ MATCHES

**** MATCHES

***¾ MATCHES

***½ MATCHES

***¼ MATCHES

*** MATCHES

The Rock vs. Jeff Jarrett
East Lansing, MI   10.04.98

Ken Shamrock & D'Lo Brown
vs. Mankind & X-Pac
Milwaukee, WI   10.19.98

HALL OF SHAME

THE WORST MATCHES OF THE YEAR

-***** MATCHES

-**** MATCHES

-*** MATCHES

-** MATCHES

-* MATCHES

DUD

The Headbangers vs. Dan Severn & Owen Hart
Des Moines, IA   08.23.98

Billy Gunn vs. 8-Ball vs. Skull
Hamilton, Canada   09.27.98

THE STORY SO FAR...

5* SHOWS
N/A

THE BEST SHOWS
N/A

GOOD SHOWS
N/A

WORTH A LOOK
10.25.98   48
11.22.98   48

DECIDEDLY AVERAGE SHOWS
12.20.98   39
12.27.98   39
09.20.98   38
10.04.98   38
11.15.98   37
09.13.98   35
08.23.98   31
09.27.98   31

BAD SHOWS
12.13.98   29
08.09.98   27
10.11.98   26
10.18.98   26
08.30.98   22
12.06.98   21
11.29.98   20

THE WORST SHOWS
09.06.98   18
08.02.98   17
08.16.98   17
11.08.98   16
11.01.98   11

SCORE AVERAGE SO FAR...
1998: 28.8

HIGHEST RATED
1998: 48   (10.25.98)

LOWEST RATED
1998:   11   (11.01.98)

HEAT VS RAW HEAD-TO-HEAD SCORES

HEAT	RAW
08.02.98 (17)	08.03.98 (48)
08.09.98 (27)	08.10.98 (48)
08.16.98 (17)	08.17.98 (67)
08.23.98 (31)	08.17.98 (95)
08.30.98 (22)	09.05.98 (32)
09.06.98 (18)	09.12.98 (24)
09.13.98 (35)	09.14.98 (74)
09.20.98 (38)	09.21.98 (34)
09.27.98 (31)	09.28.98 (43)
10.04.98 (38)	10.05.98 (51)
10.11.98 (26)	10.12.98 (61)
10.18.98 (26)	10.19.98 (51)
10.25.98 (48)	10.26.98 (14)
11.01.98 (11)	11.02.98 (39)
11.08.98 (16)	11.09.98 (32)
11.15.98 (37)	11.16.98 (16)
11.22.98 (48)	11.23.98 (8)
11.29.98 (20)	11.30.98 (32)
12.06.98 (21)	12.07.98 (36)
12.13.98 (29)	12.14.98 (71)
12.20.98 (39)	12.21.98 (63)
12.27.98 (39)	12.28.98 (49)

Heat: 4   Raw: 18

HEAT RECAP SUMMARY

The following is a tally made up of the winners of the awards given at the end of each show as part of The Heat Recap.

MATCH OF THE NIGHT
1. Edge   4
1. Brian Christopher   4
1. Ken Shamrock   4
4. X-Pac   3
4. Jeff Jarrett   3
4. The Hardy Boyz   3
4. Gangrel   3

MOST ENTERTAINING
1. Mankind   4
2. Matt Hardy   3
3. Jeff Hardy   2
3. The Rock   2
3. Vince McMahon   2

LEAST ENTERTAINING
1. Shane McMahon   7
2. DOA   3
2. Tiger Ali Singh 3

Printed in Great Britain
by Amazon